D1272555

Ballad of the Hidden Dragon

(*Liu Chih-yüan chu-kung-tiao*)

Translated with an Introduction by

M. DOLEŽELOVÁ-VELINGEROVÁ

and

J. I. CRUMP

CLARENDON PRESS · OXFORD

1971

*Oxford University Press, Ely House, London W.*1

GLASGOW NEW YORK TORONTO MELBOURNE WELLINGTON
CAPE TOWN IBADAN NAIROBI DAR ES SALAAM LUSAKA ADDIS ABABA
DELHI BOMBAY CALCUTTA MADRAS KARACHI LAHORE DACCA
KUALA LUMPUR SINGAPORE HONG KONG TOKYO

146235

895.11

B188

PRINTED IN GREAT BRITAIN
BY LUND HUMPHRIES

TÁTOVI A MÁMĚ
Milena

PREFACE

Chu-kung-tiao means 'various modes'. But to me, *chu-kung-tiao* has meant in addition various modes of pleasure which I experienced reading, studying and translating these charming *chantefables* of Chinese story-tellers.

I shall never forget my happy apprenticeship with *chu-kung-tiao* under the guidance of Professor Wu Hsiao-ling. Though very busy with his own work at the Institute of Literature in Peking, he always found time to wander with me through markets and theatres explaining the secrets of story-telling, or to spend hours poring over my books cheerfully helping to decipher the riddles of *chu-kung-tiao* language. If I have understood not only the meaning of the text, but also its message, it is to Professor Wu's credit.

My most sincere thanks are due to my teacher, Professor Jaroslav Průšek. It was he who showed me how to understand Chinese literature better. His work and his personal advice revealed to us, his disciples, not only the importance of Chinese popular literature, but also the high intellectual reward awaiting the patient student at the end of this little travelled road.

I shall always be grateful to Professor James I. Crump for his spirited enthusiasm in preparing our translation, for the unrivalled fun we had transposing with great gusto the dry and academic Czech of my draft into his succulent and playful English, but mainly for his most valuable assistance in clearing up doubtful points both in my introduction and in my translation.

For the generous sponsorship of the Center for Chinese Studies, University of Michigan, where I was Research Associate for the academic year 1967–8, I am deeply grateful and I hope that this, the final product of that year, meets with their approval.

Finally, I thank my husband Lubomír for his understanding and patience while enduring neglect by his *bas-bleu* wife. Without his encouragement this book could never have reached completion.

Toronto 1969.   M.D.-V.

COLLABORATOR'S PREFACE

A collaborator usually has no business inflicting a preface on anyone, but the special circumstances of this book's composition demand one. A number of years ago the author and I (because of similarity of interests and a congeniality of natures) began a lighthearted project which involved turning some of her valuable dissertation into English. It quickly became apparent that we got more enjoyment from doing *Liu Chih-yüan chu-kung-tiao* which she had read and worked on but had never turned into a formal translation. At first my job consisted entirely of converting the untamed, Slavic exuberance of the author's English into something far duller but more conventional to the eye of an average English reader. As I grew accustomed to the *chu-kung-tiao*'s style I was able to contribute a few suggestions and corrections but almost everything I know about the history and form of the genre I learned from the author and this book.

When the University of Michigan's Center for Chinese Studies showed interest in the work and generously sponsored further research on the subject, I was already involved to such an extent that the author insisted my name be given equal billing with hers. I was old enough to realize that she would have the final say, so I asked only to be given a place in which to set things straight – hence the collaborator's preface.

Milena Doleželová-Velingerová is the author of this book. She did all the research and is to be credited with all the insights it contains. I have ridden herd on the English of the introduction and tried to turn the verse of the translation into a kind of rhythmic language which, we hope, will suggest a few of the complicated and varied metric forms of the original. Our translated song sections are largely sprung rhythm in a stress tetrameter: many different kinds of metric feet are used but an attempt has been made to keep most lines close to four stressed beats. This is done not only because one of the most popular line lengths in *ch'ü* metre is four beats but also because readers of English verse on the whole will feel, we think, more at home with a roughly regular beat than they would with long and short verses made to vary with the line length of the original. We have used rhyme regularly in the 'codas' and occasionally throughout the text simply to remind the reader that the original *is* rhymed verse – 'codas' are not more frequently rhymed in the Chinese than are any other stanzas.

Ann Arbor, 1970   J.I.C.

CONTENTS

INTRODUCTION

I

In China, as in other Asian countries, the art of story-telling has been a very important component of national culture.

It was and still is neither more nor less than a form of popular entertainment, but a Chinese story-teller had in the past much the same cultural function in the everyday life of the illiterate Chinese commoner that mass media have today all over the world. Through his ballads he brought news to remote places, told romantic stories old and new, drawn from the otherwise closed book, taught how history was made by brave heroes in cruel wars and battles, and showed how saints, religious and political, lived and reached their goals. Thanks almost entirely to the story-teller the Chinese man in the street gained a surprisingly intimate knowledge of his own literature and history and was rapidly made aware of new ideas.

Chinese story-telling is always a homogeneous compound of several artistic components. Its basic feature is, of course, the oral presentation of a story to a large audience. The story is told or sung in vivid, colloquial language and often accompanied by a musical instrument. Sometimes miming is a required part of storyteller's representation, while a phenomenal memory and improvisational skill are taken for granted.

Since singing, performing, miming, playing instruments, improvisation, and sometimes musical composition are the accepted requirements of the story-tellers' art, long years of apprenticeship are needed to reach perfect mastery of this unique artistic craft. A well-trained and successful Chinese storyteller is seldom an amateur performing simply for the audience's pleasure; he is a professional who earns his livelihood with his craft and artistry.[1]

When the art of story-telling began in China is still the subject of research. Some Chinese scholars are convinced that it was not until the tenth century A.D. – the first recorded compositions of Chinese story-

[1] The professionalism of Chinese story-tellers is well treated and analysed in the following two studies by V. Hrdličková: 'Some Observations on the Chinese Art of Storytelling', *Acta Universitatis Carolinae, Philologica*, 3, 1964, 53–78 and 'The Professional Training of Chinese Storytellers and the Story-tellers' Guilds', *Archiv Orientální*, 33 (1965), 225–48.

tellers are both by plot and form closely related to the early Chinese translations of Buddhist *sūtras*. Others have claimed that it originated much earlier, possibly in the second century B.C. However long ago Chinese story-telling began, its artistic appeal and the warm welcome from its audience allowed it to develop a tradition which continues unbroken to the present. The story-teller's literature we have left to us today is but a small part of the whole because most compositions were neither written down nor recorded in any other way.

There are three forms in which story-tellers' compositions are known today: 1. Oral compositions (with no written version except for verbatim records of folklorists). 2. Brief notes used by story-tellers to jog their memory before or during the performance – they are the merest skeleton of the story; bones which have to be given life through the story-teller's narration. 3. Products of a professionally skilled author who may have written them to perform and interpret himself or, more likely, for another performer. They often survive in several different printed versions which seem to have been designed for literate audiences and in this form they must be considered independent works of art appealing to the reader directly without benefit of oral realization. (A sub-group consists of literary products done *in the manner* of the story-teller but which were always meant to be read, never to be performed. These we can call imitations.)

One should treat the third type of story-teller's composition, which is potentially an independent work of art, as one would any other literary work of art. Classes 1 and 2 are not suited to such analysis, because no example can exist independent of a narrator's interpretation.

In the past, Chinese literati considered all of this literature to be a marginal artistic product with low, if any, aesthetic value. Therefore, seldom was it an object of either their collection or their systematic interest. Not until the twenties of this century did Cheng Chen-to, Lu Hsün, Hu Shih, Sun K'ai-ti, A Ying, and others address themselves to it and point out its artistic significance and importance for literary, historical, and sociological studies.

Now, forty years later, the situation has changed completely. This literature is being studied intensively not only in China, but in Japan, France, the Soviet Union and, of course, in Czechoslovakia and the United States.[1]

---

[1] An extensive bibliography of studies on Chinese story-tellers' literature written in Chinese, Japanese, and western languages is to be found in J. Průšek's *The Origins and the Authors of the hua-pen*, Academia, Prague, 1967, esp. pp.114–40.

II

Towards the end of the eleventh century there appeared a new element in the development of Chinese story-teller literature, a special form called *chu-kung-tiao* ('various modes'). It flourished greatly under the Chin dynasty of the Ju–chen and during the Yüan era. By the Ming period it began to be less popular and during the fifteenth century it seems to have become largely entertainment for a reading public.

The *chu-kung-tiao* belongs to that large group of story-tellers' ballads in which prose and verse alternate, but its verse was sung, while its prose was narrated. When a poem appeared amidst the sung and the narrated parts, it was probably chanted. The *chu-kung-tiao* was a solo performance accompanied by a percussion or string instrument. It was most often a ballad of epic length and character, the action generally being condensed in and carried forward only by prose, while the sung portions (called *ch'ü*) expanded the prose by ornamenting it. The story was told in the third person through the eye of an omnipresent story-teller.

The sung part of any *chu-kung-tiao* consists of a large number of tunes (*ch'ü-tiao*) succeeding each other according to fixed musical rules. Groups of tunes belonging to the same mode (*kung-tiao*) were assembled into a 'suite' (*t'ao-shu*) to make a musical unit for which different words were supplied by each story-teller. The *chu-kung-tiao* suite is a relatively short affair compared to its dramatic counterpart. In *Liu Chih-yüan chu-kung-tiao*, for example, most suites consist of a single tune and its coda, a concluding form of the tune. In another *chu-kung-tiao*, the *Hsi-hsiang chi*, three tunes and a coda appears to be the most favoured pattern for a suite. In keeping with its title, 'various modes'. a suite belonging to mode *A* was followed by one in mode *B* or *C* and so on.

Musical tradition distinguished not only which tunes belonged to what mode, but also what positions they could occupy in a suite. For example, tune 1 could be included in the suite only in first position, while tune 2 could be any *except* the first in the suite.[1]

Because of our scanty knowledge of medieval Chinese music we do not know why any particular mode or tune alternated with another one. However, *chu-kung-tiao* music seems to have been both flexible and versatile and should have demanded a good deal of musical skill and training of the *chu-kung-tiao* composer and performer.

The *ch'ü-tiao* (tunes) of *chu-kung-tiao* were composed neither strictly

[1] A detailed analysis of *chu-kung-tiao* musical form is given by Yeh Ch'ing-ping, 'Chu-kung-tiao ti t'i-chih' in *Hsüeh-shu chi-k'an*, 5.3 (1956), 26–54.

following the rules of the earlier (Sung dynasty) *tz'u* nor those of the later (Yüan dynasty) *ch'ü*, but musically and prosodically they seem often to represent a developmental stage *between* these two forms.[1] This is brought about primarily by the particular time *chu-kung-tiao* emerged: *tz'u* had almost become outdated or out of vogue while *ch'ü* were not yet fully established and mastered by story-tellers and dramatists. There seems to have been a freer attitude in *chu-kung-tiao* toward musical rules and possibly a more liberal use of language. The story-teller used larger amounts of colloquial speech with its clichés, local expressions, and grammatical peculiarities as part of his verse than either Sung *tz'u* or Yüan *ch'ü*,[2] though his use of *ch'en-tzu* is not as extensive as Yüan drama.

The one rule strictly observed had to do with rhyme. The suite was not only a musical unit, but a prosodic one as well. Rhyme (or asso-nance) was inserted in all prescribed positions and it had always to be the same rhyme throughout any given suite. When the mode changed and a different suite began a different rhyme had to be employed.

The prose passages furnished flexibility amid the complicated musi-cal-prosodic system of *chu-kung-tiao*. When prose appeared between two different suites it could nullify the demand for alternation of modes and rhymes. That is, the same mode and the same rhyme could be used in two successive suites as long as a prose section was inserted between them. The *chu-kung-tiao* authors, however, seldom took advantage of this kind of tolerance. Too frequent use of prose ran the risk of distort-ing the distinctive feature of *chu-kung-tiao* – its modal variety.

The *chu-kung-tiao* musical convention is usually considered the most significant fore-runner of Yüan dramatic structure. Thematically and stylistically Yüan drama (which represents a high point in traditional Chinese musical-dramatic art) is the inheritor of the entire body of story-teller's literature but the musical and prosodic shape of this later genre is derived primarily from *chu-kung-tiao*. The suite as a musical and prosodic unit was incorporated into drama structure and there performed the same basic function it had in *chu-kung-tiao*. The differ-ence between the *chu-kung-tiao* suite and that of the drama lies mainly in the quantity of tunes used. While the number of tunes in *chu-kung-tiao* suites was relatively small and modes alternated frequently, in

[1] See Wang Kuo-wei, *Sung, Yüan hsi-ch'ü k'ao*, Shanghai, Liu i shu-chü 1932, pp.40–1.
[2] See Yeh Ch'ing-ping, 'Chu-kung-tiao tsai wen-hsüeh shih shang ti ti-wei' in: *Ta-lu tsa-chih*, Vol.10, No.7, pp.3–5.

Yüan drama a suite encompasses an entire act so that each act is in a single mode from beginning to end. Rules concerning the use of rhyme are similar in both genres because rhyme does not change within a suite but any two contiguous suites will usually have different rhymes.

III

Only three, or possibly four, *chu-kung-tiao* texts have been preserved:

1. *Liu Chih-yüan chu-kung-tiao*[1] (*Chu-kung-tiao* about Liu Chih-yüan) by an unknown author. The text dates from the Chin Dynasty (1115–1234) and there is extant only one copy of the original. The original is a woodblock print which came from a workshop in the region of P'ing-yang in Shansi province and was found by the Russian archaelogical expedition of 1907–8 led by Petr Kuzmitch Kozlov (1863–1935). It remained in the Leningrad Oriental Institute until April 1958 when the Soviet Government made the People's Republic of China a gift of this priceless volume and it is now kept in the Peking National Library.

The *Liu Chih-yüan chu-kung-tiao* is incomplete. Of a total of twelve chapters there remain only the first, second, and the beginning of the third chapter, the major part of chapter eleven and all of the last chapter. The subject of the narrative is Liu Chih-yüan, first Emperor of the Later Han (947–50), a short-lived house founded during the chaotic period of the Five Dynasties. What we have of the story deals exclusively with Liu Chih-yüan's youth before he became Emperor. The first three chapters describe the bitter lot of the Liu family: his father, a soldier, was killed in battle, his widowed mother fled famine with her two little sons and later re-married. After a falling-out with his half-brothers, Liu Chih-yüan leaves home, meets a village girl, Li San-niang, and marries her. The ballad then relates his second marriage to the daughter of a military dignitary and his career as a soldier. In chapters eleven and twelve we read of the happy reunion of Liu Chih-yüan and his first wife after a separation of thirteen years and about the gathering of the whole Liu family whose numerous members had been scattered all over the country.

2. *Hsi-hsiang chi chu-kung-tiao* (Story of the Western Chamber) by Tung Chieh-yüan (Master Tung) written towards the end of the twelfth century is a version of China's most popular love story. The tale of the beauty Ying-ying and student Chang was later adapted and

---

[1] We do not know the actual title of this ballad. The cover of the original is missing and the title is only alluded to in the text.

became extremely popular through Wang Shih-fu's long *tsa-chü* (Yüan drama) *Hsi-hsiang chi*. As an indication of its success, *Hsi-hsiang chi chu-kung-tiao* still exists in seven different versions.

It is Professor Crump's opinion, shared by at least one Chinese scholar,[1] that the *Liu Chih-yüan* is the *only* genuine market-place and street *chu-kung-tiao* in existence. He concludes that *Hsi-hsiang chi's* elegance and literary appeal marks it as the production of an educated professional composer for an audience of his fellow craftsman or some other limited and highly literate group.

3. *T'ien-pao i-shih chu-kung-tiao* (*Chu-kung-tiao* of the T'ien-pao era), the author of which is Wang Po-ch'eng, a playwright who wrote Yüan *tsa-chü* around 1276. This *chu-kung-tiao* has been preserved in fragments only but tells the famous story of the T'ang Emperor, Ming-huang and his favourite, Yang Kuei-fei.[2]

It is probable that a very small part of another *chu-kung-tiao* is preserved in the prologue of the earliest *nan-hsi* play, the *Chang Hsieh chuang-yüan* (Chang Hsieh the Graduate)[3] by an unknown author of Sung times. It is not certain, however, whether this text is an authentic fragment of *chu-kung-tiao* or whether it was simply a whim of the playwright to construct a prologue to his drama in the *chu-kung-tiao* form which was very popular then.

IV

Since those who could leave us records of story-tellers seldom cared to, we know almost nothing about authors and performers. However,

---

[1] See *Hua-pen hsieh-tzu hui-shuo* by Chuang Yin, Taiwan, 1965, p.58.

[2] The *T'ien-pao i-shih chu-kung-tiao* fragment is estimated to represent only a fourth of the whole ballad. Only the sung parts (tunes *ch'ü*, arranged by *kung-tiao* in suites) are preserved, scattered in various collections of model *ch'ü* tunes. The most important source of them is *Yung-hsi yüeh-fu*. Some of the tunes may be found also in *T'ai-ho cheng-yin p'u*, *Pei-tz'u kuang-cheng p'u* and *Chiu-kung ta ch'eng p'u*.

Three Chinese scholars have tried to reconstruct *T'ien-pao i-shih chu-kung-tiao*; Cheng Chen-to in his 'Sung, Chin, Yüan chu-kung-tiao k'ao' (see Bibliography), Jen Erh-pei (his manuscript prepared for publishing by K'ai-ming shu-tien Publishing house was burnt during the Japanese attack on Shanghai in 1937), and Chao Ching-shen (in *Hsüeh-shu*, 3 (1940), 123–56). Kuraishi Takeshirō's reconstruction remains, as far as I know, in manuscript.

[3] *Chang Hsieh chuang-yüan chu-kung-tiao* is preserved in the prologue to the *nan-hsi* drama *Chang Hsieh chuang-yüan* recorded in the 13,991st volume of the *Yung-lo ta-tien* Encyclopedia. This volume, discovered by chance in London in 1920, was reprinted in 1931 under the title *Yung-lo ta-tien hsi-wen san-chung* and later in Shanghai 1954 in the drama collection *Ku-pen hsi-ch'ü ts'ung-k'an*, 1st collection.

a considerable number of *chu-kung-tiao* composers' names are preserved by chance in various historical records. It seems *chu-kung-tiao* enjoyed an immense vogue for a time and its audiences often included the literati who wrote historical records.

By tradition one K'ung San-chuan (K'ung the Learned) is spoken of as the creator and first composer of *chu-kung-tiao*. It is said he hailed from Tse-chou in Shansi province and performed *chu-kung-tiao* in Pien-liang (today's K'ai-feng-fu) during the second half of the eleventh century. None of his ballads is recorded by title, but they must have been very popular for one record tells us that even the literati knew his 'old tales' by heart.[1]

This unusual popularity of *chu-kung-tiao* as early as the eleventh century casts a good deal of doubt upon the tradition of K'ung San-chuan as creator of the *chu-kung-tiao* form but it is common enough to find a name singled out as *the* creator of a form. By tradition, Kuan Han-ch'ing is considered the father of Yüan drama and Lo Kuan-chung the 'creator' of the Chinese novel. But we know the origins of both drama and novel were far earlier than these men and literary genres are seldom, if ever, created full-blown by an individual.

Chronologically the next *chu-kung-tiao* composer would be Chang Wu-niu (1131–62) who was known primarily for his *chuan-tz'u* (another kind of musical performance having much in common with *chu-kung-tiao*). He is said to have composed a *chu-kung-tiao* for the story of the student Shuang Chien and the courtesan Su Hsiao-ch'ing. This particular love story (which by Ming times seems to have been supplanted by the story of Ying-ying) was very popular during Yüan times. About thirty years after Chang Wu-niu, a certain Shang Tao (T. Sheng-shu) did another recension of the ballad of Shuang Chien, and some time about 1260 Shih Chün-pao mentions the same story in his drama *Chu-kung-tiao Feng-yüeh tzu-yün t'ing*,[1] which is still extant (*WP* 20).

---

[1] The prime source for K'ung San-chuan's activity is *Pi-chi man-chih* (A.D. 1149) by Wang Cho. Here we find a note about his performance and also a statement that it was K'ung who first composed old stories in *chu-kung-tiao* form. It is said also that even literati knew his compositions by heart. (Cf. *Chung-kuo ku-tien hsi-ch'ü lun-chu chi-ch'eng*, Peking 1959, Vol.2, p. 151.)

[2] The names of Chang Wu-niu and Shang Tao are quoted in connection with *chu-kung-tiao* in two poems (*Che-ku-t'ien* and *Hsiao-pien*) by Yang Li-chai (*ca.* 1330). The poet saw performances of Chang Wu-niu's and Shang Tao's pieces (Yang called them *ch'ü*) and composed his poems to praise their beauty. (Cf. *Ch'ao-yeh hsin-sheng t'ai p'ing yüeh-fu*, Peking 1958, pp.363–5).

Without doubt the most famous *chu-kung-tiao* composer is Tung Chieh-yüan. Well known and highly esteemed during his life, his name is recorded as first among famous playwrights of the twelfth century in *Lu-kuei pu* (The Record of Ghosts). Despite his great popularity we know nothing about Tung's life except that he was an educated man. His title, *chieh-yüan* (Graduate), was given in earlier times to those who passed the imperial examination in a prefectural capital but it was also used simply to designate a literate man. But the best testimony to his learning is the language of his *chu-kung-tiao*: it is rich, sophisticated, and full of literary and historical allusions.

Wang Po-ch'eng (second half of the thirteenth century), mentioned above as the author of one of the preserved *chu-kung-tiao* fragments, is the last recorded composer of *chu-kung-tiao*.

In addition to this bare chronology of *chu-kung-tiao* composers we also find in historical records indications of their social position. Apparently *chu-kung-tiao* composition developed in a milieu of well-known, cultivated professional artists who were a respected part of the entertainment world of large cities and were honoured as such. The *performers* were another thing entirely: despite the record of high praise for their skill in rendering *chu-kung-tiao* they were the outcasts of Chinese society as has so often been the case with entertainers.

In a Yüan dynasty text (there are several versions) called *Ch'ing-lou chi* (a Collection of Personalities from the Gay Quarters)[1] we discover that courtesan-entertainers were the most frequent performers of *chu-kung-tiao*. To be sure, ladies of this profession often made up the bulk of other types of dramatic troupes as well, but it is noteworthy that with the exception of K'ung the Learned, all the names we know to be associated with the performance of *chu-kung-tiao* are women.

Chu-kung-tiao performances were accompanied by little drums, gongs, and bamboo castanets. Later, from the fourteenth century on, stringed instruments were used and this change in musical instruments seems to signal the beginning of the decline of *chu-kung-tiao*.

The point of origin and centre of early *chu-kung-tiao* development

---

[1] *Chung-kuo ku-tien hsi-ch'ü lun-chu chi-ch'eng*, Peking 1959, Vol.2, pp.19 ff. Women *chu-kung-tiao* artists are listed in the following: *I-chien chih* by Hung Mai (1123–1202), part *chih yi*, 6.5a; *Wu-lin chiu shih* (ca.1290) (cf. *Tung-ching meng-hua-lu, wai ssu chung*, Shanghai 1957, p.459 and *Meng-liang lu* (ca.1274), ibid., p.310).

In these documents the girls performing *chu-kung-tiao* are often cited by name – a sign of their popularity. Here we find also references to the accompanying musical instruments and places where *chu-kung-tiao* were performed.

appears to have been Shansi province in northern China. K'ung San-chuan, traditional originator of the form, was supposed to have come from Tse-chou in that province and the block-print original of *Liu Chih-yüan chu-kung-tiao* was discovered in the region. Perhaps the most convincing proof of *chu-kung-tiao* provenience, however, is furnished by analysis of the rhyme system in both *Liu Chih-yüan* and *Hsi-hsiang chi*.

In most northern Chinese dialects, words ending in the nasal *-n* make one rhyme group, while words ending in the velar nasal *-ng* belong to another. In Shansi dialect, however, both become simply general nazalization with no distinctive articulation and the two classes rhyme with each other.

The fact that both of the early extant *chu-kung-tiao* show continuous substitution of *-n* and *-ng* rhymes suggests that their authors grew up in, spoke, and wrote the Shansi dialect and the two *chu-kung-tiao* were originally performed in Shansi province. One reason for the emergence of *chu-kung-tiao* and then early Yüan drama in Shansi province may have been the importance of the city and prefecture of P'ing-yang. It was a cultural, political, and military centre which must have attracted story-tellers seeking large audiences and the money to be had from them.

Between the end of the eleventh and the beginning of the twelfth centuries, *chu-kung-tiao* were performed in K'ai-feng (not very far from Shansi) which was another centre of entertainment activity. There is also some record from the twelfth century indicating that *chu-kung-tiao* were performed in the Kuei-chi district, south of modern Honan. In the thirteenth century several singing girls are listed who performed *chu-kung-tiao* in Hangchow in southern Chekiang province. Hangchow became the capital of the Sung dynasty after the invasion of the Ju-chen in the north drove all Chinese cultural life south to that city. For a long time Hangchow remained the place where story-tellers gathered and were most enthusiastically welcomed.

Since the fourteenth century *chu-kung-tiao* have seldom been a part of the professional story-tellers' repertoire; performances, when given, were limited to those done under gentry patronage.

The decline of *chu-kung-tiao* was, perhaps, inevitable in the face of the popular and flourishing Yüan drama full of new musical and per-forming innovations and geared to a theatrical stage. Another reason for the decline may have been connected with the shift of the story-tellers' centres toward the south. This was not intrinsic to the develop-ment of *chu-kung-tiao* but was brought about by external causes to be found in the political life of China. In southern regions where dialects were remote from the early language of *chu-kung-tiao*, these ballads would hardly be understandable if done in the old tongue. A very important obstacle to a southern renaissance of *chu-kung-tiao* would have been the different prosodic and musical patterns beloved and used in the south but foreign to *chu-kung-tiao*. The last *chu-kung-tiao* performance we have record of was organized by a Chinese dignitary who lived in the sixteenth century.[1] However, this *mise-en-scène* was certainly more of an artificial resurrection than a genuine *chu-kung-tiao* show.

After the fifteenth century *chu-kung-tiao* ceased to exist except as written texts enjoyed by antiquarian-minded literati. All knowledge of its method of performance was either lost or neglected; even the name *chu-kung-tiao* seems to have been dropped and during the Ch'ing period they appear to have been referred to as *ch'ou-t'an tz'u*, 'songs to stringed instruments' or *hsien-so tiao*, 'songs to strings'.

The extinction of *chu-kung-tiao* as a recognized literary form was complete by the nineteenth century when Tung Chieh-yüan's *Hsi-hsiang chi chu-kung-tiao* was treated by collectors as a Yüan drama.[2] But in 1912, Wang Kuo-wei was among the first modern Chinese scholars to recognize *chu-kung-tiao* as an independent literary form.[3]

Though only three *chu-kung-tiao* ballads (and one dubious short example) survive, allusions in these texts and other written records make it possible to reconstruct the stories of some twelve others. The plots of these are usually known because of a strong tradition: some of them are still alive today in mouths of story-tellers and the rest are to be found in collections of short stories.

Three of the four preserved *chu-kung-tiao* are love stories: Tung's *Western Chamber*, Wang Po-ch'eng's '*Chu-kung-tiao* of the T'ien-pao Era', and the previously mentioned doubtful fragment preserved in the *nan-hsi* play referred to as 'Chang Hsieh, the Graduate'. The survival rate

[1] The sixteenth-century *chu-kung-tiao* performance is recorded in *Mei-hua-ts'ao t'ang pi-t'an* by Chang Yüan-chang (1554–1630). Cf. *Hsin ch'ü-yüan*, Shanghai 1940, Vol.2, 6ab.

[2] *Chu-kung-tiao* was treated as drama by Liu Shih-heng (1937), in his collection *Hui-k'o ch'uan-chü*, and by T'ao Lo-ch'in who published *Hsi-hsiang chi chu-kung-tiao* as a *ch'uan-ch'i* as late as 1924. Also, Paul Pelliot considered *Liu Chih-yüan chu-kung-tiao* a drama in his article 'Les Documents chinois trouvés par la Mission Kozlov à Khara-khoto', *Journal Asiatique*, Onzième Série, 3 (1914), 503–18.

[3] Wang Kuo-wei's recognition of *chu-kung-tiao* as an independent literary form is to be found in *Wang Kuo-wei hsi-ch'ü lun-wen chi*, Peking, 1957, pp.45–6.

itself implies that most *chu-kung-tiao* were love stories and other information bears this speculation out. For example, in the introduction to Wang Po-ch'eng's *T'ien-pao i-shih chu-kung-tiao* the author alludes to another *chu-kung-tiao* which later became famous as a drama under the title of *P'i-p'a chi* (Record of the Lute). In addition, there are eight more love stories done into *chu-kung-tiao* form mentioned in the prologue to Tung Chieh-yüan's *Hsi-hsiang chi chu-kung-tiao*:[1] *Ts'ui T'ao feng tz'u-hu* (Ts'ui T'ao Meets a Tigress), *Cheng-tzu yü yao-hu* (Cheng-tzu Meets a Fox-demon), *Ching-ti yin yin-p'ing* (The Silver Pitcher from the Bottom of the Well), *Shuang nü tou fu* (Two Women Fight over a Husband), *Ch'ien-nü li-hun* (How Ch'ien Nü Left her Soul), *Yeh chiang Ts'ui Hu* (Ts'ui Hu Begs a Drink), *Shuang Chien Yü-chang ch'eng* (Shuang Chien in Yü-chang Town) and finally, *Liu Yi ch'uan shu* (Liu Yi Delivers a Letter).

With the exception of 'Shuang Chien in Yü-chang Town' – a story treated in the *chu-kung-tiao* composed by Chang Wu-niu and later re-worked by Shang Tao – the story-lines of these eight *chu-kung-tiao* appear in the Sung dynasty collection *T'ai-p'ing kuang-chi* (T'ai-p'ing Miscellany), which contains thousands of anecdotes and brief pieces of fiction written by literati in the literary language. Most of these pieces (they are known loosely as *pi-chi* or 'jottings') were written during the T'ang and Five Dynasties era and almost without exception deal with thaumaturgic material. The most popular of them concern those demons and spirits which take on the form of ravishing beauties in order to seduce good, though somewhat credulous, men. They are replete with wild passions and mysteries but generally conclude on a happy note.

The preponderance of love stories in *chu-kung-tiao* ballads is certainly striking. Remember, however, where *chu-kung-tiao* were usually performed. *Chu-kung-tiao* more than any other story-teller form were produced in those entertainment houses of the gay quarters where the entertainment was not limited to theatrical shows and they were told by professionals whose first profession was far older than story-telling. The milieu where *chu-kung-tiao* found such favour probably made its influence felt on the choice of story and shaped many of the motifs common to *chu-kung-tiao* ballads: descriptions of feminine charms,

---

[1] To enumerate stories *not* to be performed and acquaint the audience with the theme of the ballad actually being done only at the very end of the prologue was a favourite story-tellers' trick. Because it was indulged in here we have these eight titles preserved.

dilation upon love games, emphasis on female characters, and admiration for passion that surmounts all obstacles.

Among the preserved *chu-kung-tiao*, *Liu Chih-yüan* is the only story of a historical hero. It is believed, however, that at least one other *chu-kung-tiao* entitled *Pa-wang*[1] dealt with the history of Hsiang Yü, the famous Ch'u rebel against the Ch'in dynasty during the third century B.C. There is no evidence that detective or religious *chu-kung-tiao* were ever composed – indeed, a detective story would demand a complicated plot structure which the *chu-kung-tiao* form would find almost impossible to support and a religious *chu-kung-tiao* told by a sing-song girl in a *bagnio* would always run the risk of becoming a farce.

In the case of *Liu Chih-yüan* I believe the composer did not draw his details directly from the *History of the Five Dynasties* but rather from a number of pre-existing story-tellers' treatments of Liu Chih-yüan. In the case of the romantic themes, however, it seems logical to assume that the composer of *chu-kung-tiao* went directly to sources in the literary language such as *T'ai-p'ing Kuang-chi* (the majority of composers of whom we have record seem to have been sufficiently literate to do this), for stories of romantic love seem not to have existed anywhere except in such collections of literary-language anecdotes. However, the *Hsi-hsiang chi chu-kung-tiao* is proof that the migration of themes from literary stories done by the literati to the story-tellers' popular ballads was a complex process. The story-teller would use any theme but he always altered and arranged it to suit his taste, the interest of his audience and the requirements of his form.

V

In the case of a literary work of art destined for a reader there is an interpretation gap between sender (author) and receiver (reader). The work may be accepted as the author intended it; it may be slightly misinterpreted; or if the distance in time between writer and reader is sufficiently great, the original message of the work may be substantially changed because the receiver's social and temporal framework is so different. The existence of a written literary work is, however, not essentially and primarily dependent on the reader's reaction – sometimes the originator does not even reckon with him (as may happen for instance, with a diary, or poems never intended for publication, etc.).

---

[1] The historical *chu-kung-tiao* 'Pa-wang' is cited in *Wu-lin chiu-shih* (cf. *Tung-ching meng-hua lu, wai ssu chung*, p. 509). Another *chu-kung-tiao* is listed in the same place under the title *Kua ts'e erh*. Its contents are totally unknown.

It is quite otherwise with an art which exists primarily in oral form. In the case of a Chinese story-teller ballad, the relationship between the originator and his audience is so essential and so tight that the existence and the shape of the production is directly dependent on the audience's reaction. The interpretation gap between the creator and the reader has, in the case of Chinese story-teller literature, disappeared because the story-teller is forced by his profession to foresee his client's expectations, wishes, and moods and to react to them, though they may be very changeable indeed. Either the story-teller knows and reacts to his audience with skill, is successful, and earns his livelihood, or he misjudges them and fails. So in a certain sense audience reaction is not a passive but an active, creative factor in the Chinese story-telling.[1]

The *chu-kung-tiao* ballad had the same requirement as any other story-teller performance: to entertain the audience, to lead them from the everyday reality of life into the beguiling world of fiction. It gave them what they wanted – the colourfulness they could not find in the grey of daily life.

Let us not ask now what the *chu-kung-tiao* author introduced into his ballad to entertain his audience, but *how* and by what means he reached his goal. As with other relatively simple forms (fairy-tales, myths), analysis of a single specimen tends only to distort. Structure and components emerge clearly only when several representatives of the same form are compared with one another. *Liu Chih-yüan chu-kung-tiao* is here the prime source for analysis, but *Hsi-hsiang chi chu-kung-tiao* is very useful to check with our observations. It is my hope that this comparison will illuminate not only the common features distinguishing *chu-kung-tiao* as a genre, but also some of the differences traceable to idiosyncrasies of the authors.[2]

Chu-kung-tiao authors did not attempt to invent new stories, they took over themes from earlier sources. The art of the Chinese story-teller was deeply traditional and conservative – a very small number of themes can be found repeated in story-tellers' productions separated by centuries. In the Middle Ages, both in China and in Europe there

[1] See A. B. Lord, *Singer of Tales*, Atheneum, N.Y.C. 1968. His singers, being truly unlettered and only semi-professional, present a somewhat different case but the effect of the audience is the same.
[2] We will not take into consideration *T'ien-pao i-shih chu-kung-tiao* because it is much more fragmentary than *Liu Chih-yüan chu-kung-tiao* and is an atypical example of *chu-kung-tiao* form, showing very strong formal influence from Yüan drama.

was little interest in thematic originality[1] in the modern sense of the term. Originality was neither appreciated nor valued because the medieval poet was not expected to think independently. Novelty of theme was usually something undesirable, so the author tried to stick closely to a traditional model.

But did the story-teller consistently follow the traditional model or did he always strive to modify it, and in what degree? Doubtless this question could be well answered if we had detailed analyses of a number of story-tellers' productions in which we could trace and isolate the variables of the individual story-teller's additions from the invariables of the traditional themes. For this introduction, however, our goal is more modest – we would like to demonstrate how a particular theme was developed and how it took on the form it assumes in the *chu-kung-tiao*. It is also our hope that information about the story itself will enhance the reader's enjoyment of the translation.

Since the protagonist of *Liu Chih-yüan chu-kung-tiao* was a historic personality, it is of some interest to know how his life and career were described in the historical records and whether such sources had any influence on the story-tellers' compositions which used the Liu Chih-yüan story.

Liu Chih-yüan's life appears in an official biography in the *Han-shu*, the dynastic records of the Han dynasty (A.D. 936–43),[2] but because his reign as Emperor lasted only three and a half years, the orthodox historical record is focused primarily on Liu Chih-yüan's successful career as a skilful general and governor of the rich area of Ping-chou and dwells on his clever stratagems against both his own ruler, the Emperor of the Chin dynasty, and the invading Khitans. Except for a brief comment on the young Liu Chih-yüan's appearance and character, there is not a single episode related to his youth.

As a story-teller theme, the story of Liu Chih-yüan probably appeared first in the collection of story-tellers' popular chronicles called *Hsin-pien Wu tai-shih p'ing-hua* (*P'ing-hua* on the History of the Five Dynasties, New Edition).[3] The latter half of this is mere recitation

---

[1] Modern survivals of earlier oral traditions react the same way. See Lord, op. cit., esp. Ch.4.

[2] Liu Chih-yüan's life is described in the *Han-shu* preserved in the dynastic history *Chiu Wu-tai shih* (*Po-na* esp. Chs.99 and 100). Brief comment on the young Liu Chih-yüan's appearance is in Ch.99, 1a.

[3] The collection *Hsin-pien Wu-tai shih p'ing-hua* was reprinted in Shanghai, 1954. Its dates are not clear. In the Preface of the new Shanghai edition it is stated that the chronicles were composed some time during the Sung and re-edited during

of historical facts in a style of language which we assume was under-standable to an illiterate audience. Although apparently intimately acquainted with, and anxious to adhere to his model – the official *Han-shu*[1] – the story-teller nevertheless finds suitable scope for his own expression: he lavishes all his creative ability on the youth of his hero.[2] Since the orthodox records, as we have mentioned, contained almost no information on Liu Chih-yüan's childhood and youth, the story-teller was free in that area to use both his imagination and ele-ments from other hero legends.[3]

We assume that the legend of Liu Chih-yüan existed in oral form before the *p'ing-hua*, but in the *p'ing-hua* the core of it appears for the first time in written form. Later, this core was re-used in *chu-kung-tiao* and in dramas.

The author of *Liu Chih-yüan chu-kung-tiao* goes one step further than the *p'ing-hua* author. He ignores the historical personage completely and limits the story entirely to the early years of the emperor-to-be. Here he can and does supplement the core story with numerous fic-tional episodes developed out of his own imagination fertilized by traditional legendary components.[4]

the Yüan dynasty. The story of Liu Chih-yüan is told in the particular chronicle called *Hsin-pien Wu-tai Han-shu* and this was translated by J. I. Crump in his unpublished dissertation, 'Some Problems in the Language of the Shin-bian Wuu-day shyy pyng-huah,' Vol.II (Yale University, 1949). I wish to express my thanks to the author for his kindness in lending it to me.

---

[1] We find, for example, the same description of Liu Chih-yüan's appearance, as appeared in the official records: 'He was a stern and grave fellow who was not given to talking and laughter. His complexion was dark with a purplish cast, and the whites of his eyes were prominent' (Crump's translation).

[2] A popular story-teller's device, as pointed out by Crump in 'P'ing-hua and the Early History of the San-kuo chih', *JAOS*, 71, (1951), 249–56, and in C. T. Hsia's unpublished article, 'The Military Romance' delivered at the Bermuda Conference on Chinese Literature, 1967.

[3] The popular chronicle (*p'ing-hua*) 'draws to a significant extent upon a common heritage of hero-legends irrespective of whether these legends already existed in a written form or remained in a fluid state as folklore.' This is C. T. Hsia's statement (op. cit.) about the chronicle author's general approach to a theme.

[4] The author of the *chu-kung-tiao* also pretends to be acquainted with Liu's official biography in the orthodox *Han-shu* and cites the names of Liu and his father and their places of origin in a fashion designed to make the hearer believe the story-teller had read the text. The sentences are so garbled, however, that he demonstrates in fact how *little* he knows of the historical text. He even gives the wrong character for the name of Liu's father. This is very different indeed from the *p'ing-hua* story-teller who quotes long passages from the official history verbatim.

Because the *p'ing-hua* and *chu-kung-tiao* represent two different stages in the development of the Liu Chih-yüan legend, we are able to differentiate between the components which form, so to speak, the trunk of the legend, and those details or branches added by the two authors.

In the table which follows, the centre column gives the common core of the legend abstracted from the opening sections of the *p'ing-hua* and *chu-kung-tiao*; the left-hand column gives the *p'ing-hua* deviation from the core, and the right-hand one gives the *chu-kung-tiao* variation:

P'ing-hua variant	Static Legendary Motifs	*Chu-kung-tiao* variant
Because Liu's father had died, Liu's mother asks her brother-in-law to take her son into his family. She is refused and advised to re-marry. She takes Mu-jung as her new husband.	Liu Chih-yüan's family becomes poor. Liu's mother seeks a solution from the miserable situation by marrying.	Because Liu's father, a warrior, is killed in battle, Liu's mother flees with her two sons to 'friendlier lands' and re-marries Mu-jung. She bears him two sons.
Because Liu was good for nothing, his step-father drives him out. To placate his mother he calls him back and offers him one last opportunity: he gives him cash and sends him off to pay the taxes.	Liu leaves his home.	Liu's half-brothers mock their elder brother because of his different name. He himself decides to leave the house.
Liu loses the tax money gambling and wants it back. He fights the five youngsters participating in the game.	Liu fights during his trip.	Because an innkeeper gives Liu a meal free, he fights with a villager who behaves in a rude manner to the innkeeper.
Caught by darkness Liu spends the night on top of the outer gate of a wealthy farmer.	Liu falls asleep.	Tired, Liu takes a rest under a tree near a village.
In a dream, Li the elder, the owner of the house where Liu slept, sees a red serpent atop his gate tower.	Li, the elder, sees strange phenomena associated with Liu.	Li, the elder, goes out of the village to visit his fields and sees Liu surrounded by purple mist.

As can be readily seen from this, the stable elements in both the *p'ing-hua* and the *chu-kung-tiao* are the core of the legend, while variable elements appear in the details which slightly change and colour the traditional core. The combination and alternation of expected, stable elements with unexpected variants produces the tension in the structure of the legend which accounts both for its artistic effect and its evolution.

However, the great transformation from the *p'ing-hua* to the *chu-kung-tiao* treatment of the Liu Chih-yüan legend lies in another direction, in my opinion: the shape of the genre itself exerted the greatest influence upon the quality the legend takes on.

The *p'ing-hua* is a chronicle where the legendary elements are incorporated into a historical framework. The *chu-kung-tiao* is a romance where imaginative elements are intensified and the historical framework remains barely visible as the regulator of the succession of episodes. The romanticizing of the Liu Chih-yüan legend (begun in the *chu-kung-tiao* form) finally reaches completion in Yüan and Ming period dramas (*Pai t'u chi* and *Liu Chih-yüan pai t'u chi*) in which even the historical framework disappears and the plot is submerged by fictional elements.[1]

The rejection of historic realities and the enthusiastic exploitation of romanticism is not a peculiarity of *chu-kung-tiao* alone. The same trend in historical *hsiao-shuo* (another genre of Chinese story-teller literature developed approximately at the same time as *chu-kung-tiao*) and in later historical novels[2] reflects, in my opinion, the general change in the attitude of the folk audience toward history. The clients of story-tellers had no abiding interest in the true image of a historical hero; they would rather see him as they wished to see him.[3] They wanted their hero in a satisfactory situation whether or not such a situation occurred in reality. This, of course, hastened the creation of stereotyped heroes and formulaic situations.

---

[1] It may be of interest to mention here that the development of fairy-tales, as V. Propp observed, proceeds in the opposite direction: the fantastic elements are replaced by the realistic ones. However, as V. Propp added, this direction of development can be expected only with respect to the tales with religious (mythological) background. Cf. V. Propp, 'Transformacii volshebnyh skazok' (The Transformations of Fairy-tales), *Poetika*, Vol.4, Leningrad 1928, pp.70–89, esp. p.77.

[2] J. Průšek points out the similar transformation of a historical hero, the founder of the Sung dynasty, Chao K'uang-yin, in the *hsiao-shuo*, 'Chao t'ai-tsu ch'ien-li sung Ching-niang', (How the founder of the Chao clan escorted Ching-niang for a thousand miles), *Die Literatur des befreiten China und ihre Volks-traditionen*, Artia, Prague 1955, p.398.

[3] C. T. Hsia, op. cit.

In the case of *Hsi-hsiang chi chu-kung-tiao* the development of theme was more complicated. Tung Chieh-yüan took as his model the famous high literature short story *Ying-ying chuan* (The story of Ying-ying) by Yüan Chen (779–831) which describes the love idyll between student Chang and the beauty Ying-ying and ends with the separation of the lovers. Yüan Chen's short story is a chamber masterpiece with a fragile psychological atmosphere and is almost unique among the short stories of that era because it developed believable human beings instead of stereotyped vampires and other imaginary creatures. The feelings and emotional reactions of both principals – especially those of Ying-ying, half-child, half-woman – reflect, it is believed, the author's own experience. The theme is in no sense an epic but a sensitive description of the kindling and the death of a love.

There is an essential difference between Tung Chieh-yüan's task of re-doing his model and that of the author of *Liu Chih-yüan chu-kung-tiao*. Whereas in the latter case the legend was widely known to the story-teller's audience, Tung had no traditional core already accepted by his listeners.[1] The whole concept and especially the tragic dénouement of Yüan Chen's story did not fit the tastes of a story-teller's audience; the psychological treatment was probably too remote, and would have been found a bit boring for the story-tellers' clients. There was too little suspense in the plot to attract the listener in the street.

In order to create a successful composition from Yüan Chen's story, Tung Chieh-yüan had not only to re-do the story but to add new episodes and change details; he was forced, in fact, to transform its whole focus and structure. This transformation reflects the migration of the story from the context of high (literati) literature to the completely different literary world of the story-teller.

Tung's greatest alteration was the dénouement of Yüan Chen's short story. In the *chu-kung-tiao* version, the lovers are united in the end. This change to a 'happy ending' is in a literary sense too easy, even cheap, but it lies at the very core of Tung's transformation. He

---

[1] The earliest surviving story-teller's version of Yüan Chen's story is the *ku-tzu-tz'u* (drum story) by Chao Ling-chih (last half of the eleventh century). This was done *in the manner of* the story-teller but it is doubtful if it was ever performed in the market place. It represents a mechanical transposition of the literati's short story into the story-teller form: Yüan Chen's text remained intact, interspersed only by ten lyrical songs and framed by a prologue and epilogue by Chao Ling-chih. There is no evidence that the Yüan Chen's theme achieved popular appeal through this kind of re-doing. On the contrary, the majority of later story-tellers' compositions draw upon the Tung Chieh-yüan romance exclusively.

subordinated the individual author's experience – in the original he finds it impossible to choose his own marriage partner – to the popular wish to see the lovers reunited.

Once he has decided upon the great change of emphasis, Tung relies only on traditional, well-tried story-teller's methods of elaborating his story. He inserts new details, new episodes into it (e.g., the elaboration of a bandit attack on the monastery where Ying-ying's family and Chang are staying, the rescue of the monastery with the aid of Chang's friend, General White Horse, the mass for Ying-ying's father during which the monks gaze longingly at the beautiful maiden instead of praying). Tung's approach is different from his literati predecessor: to keep his audience's attention at all times he introduces and enlarges upon intrigues and battles instead of dilating on the psychological states of the hero the way his predecessor did.

Interestingly enough, Tung's transformation of his model reflects tendencies already observed in the *Liu Chih-yüan chu-kung-tiao*. Though the sources of the two romances and their themes differ greatly, the *results of their transformation under the pressure of the genre form are quite similar.* The audiences' desire for the romantic appears both in the successful career of Liu Chih-yüan and the happy outcome of Tung's love story. Idealization is typical for both of the *chu-kung-tiao* and is in fact a characteristic of the genre.

This brief comparison – though certainly suffering from a lack of compared specimens – allows a preliminary description of *chu-kung-tiao* as a genre of story-tellers' balladry, characterized by a tendency toward romantic idealization and exaggeration.

This *chu-kung-tiao* trait becomes even clearer when they are compared with the short stories, *hsiao-shuo*, developed at approximately the same time as *chu-kung-tiao*. As Průšek points out in his analysis,[1] the dénouement of the majority of *hsiao-shuo* is tragic. The historical ones often end with the death of the hero, others end in murder. Parricide and numerous violent misfortunes are detailed in crime stories (*kung-an hsiao-shuo*) as well as in the love stories. Průšek sees in these dénouements and moods of the *hsiao-shuo* a tendency toward realistic depiction of a cruel life. This tendency is reflected also in their portrayal of characters and milieu.

[1] Cf. J. Průšek, *Die Literatur des befreiten China und ihre Volks-traditionen*, especially Ch.V. The analysis is of several short stories from the *Ching-pen t'ung-su hsiao-shuo*, *Ch'ing-p'ing-shan-t'ang hua-pen*, *Ku-chin hsiao-shuo*, *Ching shih t'ung-yen*, and *Hsing shih heng-yen* collections.

It seems obvious that *chu-kung-tiao* – with its idealization and romantic exaggeration – represents one extreme of story-teller's literature
while *hsiao-shuo* – with its frequent use of blood and grief – represents
the other. There is nothing strange in this (similar tendencies can be
found in literature purely for entertainment almost everywhere in the
world) for these extremes appeal most readily to simple natures and
they interest audiences precisely because such events are exotic and
rarely an actual part of their everyday lives.

VI

A western reader acquainted with the modern novel is usually
struck by two aspects of Chinese traditional fiction: its constant repetition of a limited number of character types and their static, never-
developing inward life. Throughout the long growth of Chinese story-
telling and vernacular fiction, characters are most often generalized
types – the prince, the scholar, the swordsman[1] – very much in the
manner of fairy tales and the Italian *commedia dell' arte*. They seldom
change, physically or psychologically, throughout the whole story –
they are one-dimensional, monolithic. But whether the westerner's
taste may find this congenial or not is somewhat beside the point. It
need not be treated as either a defect or a limitation, but simply as a
characteristic property. In fact it seems to me that in some ways the
widespread western conviction about the mental flatness and opaque-
ness of characters in vernacular literature is captious. It is caused by an
inapposite comparison between Chinese *medieval* fiction and *modern*
western fiction where a developing inward life for characters is often
felt to be the essential element in characterization. Critics of Chinese
vernacular literature seem to forget that the concept of a developing
character who changes inwardly is quite a late arrival and is connected
in western fictional narrations with literary works where Christian

---

[1] This opinion was expressed for instance in John L. Bishop's 'Limitations in
Chinese fiction', *Studies in Chinese Literature*, Harvard University Press, Cam-
bridge, Massachusetts, 1965, pp.240–7: 'In the matter of character portrayal,
another contrast between Chinese and western fiction is apparent. Both literatures
attempt realistic portrayals of social types and the difference between them is one
of degree. Both exploit dialogue as a means of differentiating character and caste.
The novel of the West, however, explores more thoroughly the minds of characters and long familiarity with this realm has made possible whole novels which
are confined to the individual mind alone, such as those of Virginia Wolfe and
James Joyce. But to the Chinese novelist, the mental life of his fictional characters
is an area to be entered only briefly when necessary and then with timidity'
(p.245).

concepts begin to blend with late Celtic romances. (The Parsifal story of the twelfth century is an excellent example of this combination.) The psychological portrayal of characters in written (as opposed to oral) western literature waited even longer – until the seventeenth century, when psychology as a formal discipline was born.[1]

To be sure, characters with a certain amount of inward life existed a long time before psychological analysis appeared in fiction. However, as Scholes and Kellogg point out, the phenomenon did not occupy a prominent position in the structure of ancient narrative: 'A successful narrative need not emphasize the inward life and present it in detail, it must be prepared to compensate with other elements if it is to remain an object of interest to men. The Greek romances compensated with involved plotting, vivid description, an ornate rhetoric, and so did their English and French imitators of the sixteenth and seventeenth centuries.'[2]

Could *chu-kung-tiao* present the inner life of characters when the authors used 'prefabricated' types as protagonists?

In *Liu Chih-yüan chu-kung-tiao*, the hero belongs to the type 'prince – dynastic founder'. As a member of this class his appearance, behaviour, and nature are determined by a traditional mould and are in full accord with it. Like most of his confrères in vernacular novels (especially military romances) there is absolutely no attempt to draw the image of his actual historical model. On the contrary, Liu Chih-yüan is clearly 'an amalgam of myths, legend and folktale, acting within the patterns of his mythic destinies'.[3] Like many another legendary Chinese hero his destiny is forecast by a golden snake wriggling in and out his nostrils during his sleep, by purple mist and crimson glow above his head. As an emperor-to-be, he must be handsome, brave, virtuous, merciful, and a master at handling arms. Fatal dangers and his mortal enemies set upon him but he always emerges victorious because of the tutelage and protection of a celestial master or force.

In *Hsi-hsiang chi chu-kung-tiao*, Tung Chieh-yüan also utilizes traditional types made famous through the literati's short novel – the beautiful maiden, the young student, the clever maid, and a scheming old woman.

Features describing the hero's type characteristics (the genealogy,

---

[1] Cf. R. Scholes and R. Kellogg, *The Nature of Narrative*, Oxford University Press, New York 1966, pp.167 and 189.
[2] Ibid., p.171.
[3] Cf. C. T. Hsia, op. cit.

the physiognomy, and heroic attributes) are generally expressed as *direct characteristics* (those the author expressly states about the character). They formally introduce the personage to the audience and therefore they usually appear immediately after the hero enters the story.[1] Because they mirror the traditional stereotyped image of the character, the direct characteristics too, are general and stereotyped. (The stereotype is so strong that it is used even when the description will not fit the plot circumstances: e.g., Liu Chih-yüan's wife, Li San-niang, is a simple village girl, but since she belongs to the type 'beauty-heroine' she is described in the same fashion as her aristocratic counterpart from *Hsi-hsiang chi chu-kung-tiao*, Ying-ying.)

In the process of character portrayal, the statement of type qualities as direct characteristics represents the first step only. In order to flesh out the individual personality which is first formed by the traditional mould, the story-teller had to create traits which would develop a more complex, more vivid, more human character. At this point the genuine creative process of the story-teller begins.

Most often he fills out the psychology and personality of his character by *indirect characteristics* – implying the nature of a person by actions and incidents imbedded in the narrative. For instance, Liu Chih-yüan defends the harried innkeeper and he is reluctant to leave his wife even in the face of the plots her brothers devise against him. By these incidents the listeners learn that Liu has a passion for justice and is faithful as well as brave. (Tung Chieh-yüan paints the portrait of a young student totally addled by love when he details his hero's foolish behaviour during the mass given for Ying-ying's father.)

Narrative episodes implying the character of the actors are used in all story-tellers' productions, but there is a particular characteristic of the *chu-kung-tiao* which sets it apart from other narrators' compositions and makes it in some ways remarkably like its descendant, the poetic drama of the Yüan. *Chu-kung-tiao* uses detailed and poetic re-statements of incidents to reveal the intensity and quality of a character's inner feelings.

A typical example of this appears in the first chapter describing Liu Chih-yüan's anger and his fight with the villain who has treated the

---

[1] This holds true of all the characters involved in the story of *Hsi-hsiang chi chu-kung-tiao* as well as of the subordinate characters in *Liu Chih-yüan chu-kung-tiao*. Only in the case of Liu Chih-yüan is the rule slightly changed: at the beginning of the story we learn his genealogy and his presumed glorious destiny, while his physical appearance is described in the second part of the first chapter.

innocent innkeeper harshly. When the narrative episode comes to its climax we have the detailed re-statement – which tends toward hyperbole and a kind of exaltation – to emphasize the peak of the hero's mood and action. In both extant *chu-kung-tiao* compositions this hyperbole is usually dressed as an allegory and presented as the narrator's commentary. In the example under consideration Liu's anger is highlighted by the following tetrastich: 'Chih-yüan's impetus was like a dragon's surging from the uprushing waves. The bully's strength diminished like a mortally wounded tiger which has sheathed its claws.' (A similar device may be found in *Hsi-hsiang chi chu-kung-tiao* in an episode describing the battle of monks with the bandit army surrounding the monastery. Fa-ts'ung, the leader of the monks is there compared to a bull and a tiger while his horse is described as an enraged elephant.)

Since these verse re-statements are usually inserted where moods and emotions reach their peak, in *Liu Chih-yüan chu-kung-tiao* fights, battles (in Chapter 12), and intrigues carry a heavy freight of them. In Tung Chieh-yüan's romance, battle is used only once (it is an extensive one, however), its place being taken by scenes more appropriate to love stories; restless expectation and separation of the lovers, intrigues obstructing the lovers' meeting, and, of course, the sweet and secret rendezvous.

Dialogues, monologues, and inner monologues are all used to create individual characters from types. Since all three are common and since they may have developed one from the other, let us consider them as one rather than three devices.

In the dialogue, two persons are actively involved in the conversation, but sometimes person *A*, recapitulating past action, explains the reasons for his feeling or deeds to *B* who might have misunderstood them. Compare, for example, the dialogue between Liu Chih-yüan and Li San-niang during their first meeting and when they part. (In *Hsi-hsiang chi chu-kung-tiao* this kind of dialogue occurs between student Chang and the handmaiden Hung-niang.) This kind of dialogue reveals or clarifies the inward life of characters, and contributions of both parties to the dialogue are usually about equal. There is another kind of dialogue which deals with neither speaker but with a third person who usually has not yet appeared in the story or who is not known to one of the persons involved in the dialogue. This type usually describes the physical appearance of a third person. The dialogue between Liu Chih-yüan and Li San-niang about their son and those

between the monk (or the widow) and the student about Ying-ying
are examples. In this second type one speaker is the carrier of the message, the listener interrupts him only with short questions.

It is only a step from this second type of dialogue to the monologue
in *chu-kung-tiao*. The story is arranged in such a fashion that one character will be prompted to address a long monologue to another (or
others) who listen (cf. Liu Chih-yüan's monologue before Li the
Learned about his past life or Li San-niang's speech at the banquet about
her cruel treatment). The soliloquy may recapitulate action or describe
attitudes, emotions, and physical appearance of yet a third person.
When the listener disappears from the scene and the speaker is alone,
or supposes himself to be alone, his soliliquy can be called an interior
monologue.[1] In *Liu Chih-yüan chu-kung-tiao* an interior monologue
appears twice. The first describes Liu Chih-yüan's dilemma – should
he stay with his beloved Li San-niang or leave her because of his
career? The second comes when Liu Chih-yüan is offered the General's
daughter in marriage (though he already has a wife in the village). In
Hsi-hsiang chi chu-kung-tiao an interior monologue is delivered by student Chang when Ying-ying's mother breaks her promise to make her
daughter his wife and instead of a wedding she arranges only a banquet
to honour Chang and make him Ying-ying's adopted brother. In both
chu-kung-tiao the heroes feel intensely the dilemma of the situation;
they are first confused but finally decide on an act to resolve it
(Liu Chih-yüan leaves Li San-niang and marries the General's
daughter, student Chang decides to leave the place he first met Ying-
ying).

The interior monologue in both *chu-kung-tiao* seems to be confined
to the protagonist faced by a dilemma which he resolves by some
action after he has, in a sense, talked it out with himself.[2]

[1] The term interior monologue is often used indiscriminately in modern fiction.
However, Scholes and Kellogg show (p.177n) that this term can also apply to
ancient narrative literature. 'It is in narrative literature, a direct, immediate presentation of unspoken thoughts of a character without any intervening narrator
. . . One of the major developments in the history of narrative characterization is
the tendency in modern literature for interior monologue to be employed widely
and without specific occasion, while in ancient times they were used sparingly
and in fairly well specified situations.' This description of interior monologue fits
well with my observation of *chu-kung-tiao*, and I use it in the same sense.

[2] A very similar manner of characterization was used by the authors of '*roman
d'aventure*' created in France in the thirteenth century. Faith Lyons, in his book

Continued on next page

Hsiao-shuo also contain dialogues which add to the picture of a character,[1] but as far as I can observe, verse dialogues, monologues, and interior monologues which recapitulate actions and add to characterization are peculiarities of the *chu-kung-tiao* technique and proved to be a very powerful addition to the storytellers' art. The *chu-kung-tiao* monologues remind one forcefully of the monologues of Yüan drama recapitulation; lyric description and inner feeling of third persons are their hallmarks. It is reasonable to believe that *chu-kung-tiao* actively influenced the Yüan drama in this respect.

Many devices of characterization in *Liu Chih-yüan chu-kung-tiao* and *Hsi-hsiang chi chu-kung-tiao* are identical, but Tung chieh-yüan's composition differs greatly from his historical confrère in one important respect – Tung inherited a story in which the character types tend not to behave in the manner their typing required. In *Liu Chih-yüan chu-kung-tiao* for example, if the story had involved a high-born, chaste young woman she would have remained so to the end. But the central feature of *Hsi-hsiang chi chu-kung-tiao* is precisely the illicit love-idyll enjoyed by Ying-ying who by type tradition should have been retiring and chaste. Tung not only adapted non-traditional characters into his genre, but intensified their atypical features. Not only did he increase the number of episodes testifying to their particular traits, but – and this is as important as his intensification – he let his heroine act and behave atypically to the very end. The originator of the story, Yüan Chen, made his student and his beauty non-conformist, yet at the first serious obstacle (separation), they turn passive and obedient – behaviour expected of them by their society. Their love story had to end unhappily and it did – both married suitably and Ying-ying, faithful wife, later refused her first lover's request simply to visit her.

Tung's lovers found death preferable to separation at the dictates of social laws. Tung grants his lovers stout hearts, has them succeed

Continued from previous page

Les elements déscriptifs dans le roman d'aventure au XIIIe siècle (Genève, Librairie Droz 1965, p.173), gives us the following summary of their descriptive technique:

'Au morceau déscriptif qui se plaque sur le récit, ils préfèrent la description faite indirectement, plus dramatique et dynamique, qui se fond avec le récit, tout de mouvement et de vie. Nous pouvons citer tout de suite les trois moyens principaux que nos écrivains utilisent à cet effet: ils décrivent, de façon émouvante, par suggestion; ils décrivent, de façon dramatique à travers le discours direct, notamment le dialogue des personnages; ils décrivent de façon active en faisant entrer les éléments déscriptifs ainsi associés à l'action, dans l'intrigue.'

[1] Cf. J. L. Bishop, op. cit., p.245.

against great odds and rewards them with a final happy reunion. He also invented what must have been at the time a highly original personality for Ying-ying's handmaid, Hung-niang, who finally steals the entire show. Instead of being almost invisible as she was in the literatus's story and as she would have been in any traditional treatment, she arranges assignations, outwits Ying-ying's mother, offers advice, and generally makes the other characters appear feckless by comparison.

Tung could also utilize his setting exceptionally well for contrast because a Buddhist monastery is the trysting place (in the Yüan Chen version this is hardly noticed). Furthermore, battles – the most important elements of many traditional stories and often treated with supernatural solemnity – take on a wry slant in *Hsi-hsiang chi chu-kung-tiao*, where monks beat off a bandit attack armed with a variety of kitchen utensils. It is perhaps because of this humour, ingenuity and rejection of type behaviour that Ying-ying and her lover became as widely known and welcomed in the Chinese world as Romeo and Juliet are in the West.

As Viktor Shklovskij points out in his analysis of medieval European fiction,[1] a favoured method of plot structure was 'stringing together': one finished episode is threaded upon another, their string being the protagonist, who unifies them simply by taking part in all.

The plot in *chu-kung-tiao* is constructed from chapters (*chüan*) which are nearly independent wholes. Each of them is divided again into several minor plot units or episodes, which could be omitted or replaced by another if the storyteller's audience demanded it. The chapters and episodes follow each other in chronological succession and are combined into a whole by the unifying element of the hero. This narrative method resembles that of the oldest Spanish picaresque novels (e.g. *Lazarillo de Tormes*), where the succession of episodes is generated by the hero's travel in search of a career. In *Liu Chih-yüan chu-kung-tiao* the hero's adventures are informed by his predestination to become Emperor. (*Hsi-hsiang chi* is slightly different; there the hero overcomes all obstacles because of his love.) There is, however, one remarkable difference between the chapters and episodes in *chu-kung-tiao* and medieval European fiction. The *chu-kung-tiao* chapter and episode is often *not* conceived as a logical whole with a beginning, middle, and end, but is terminated by the introduction of a new and exciting event, the resolution of which is usually to be given only at the begin-

[1] V. Shklovskij, *O teorii prozy* (The Theory of Prose), Moscow, Leningrad, 1925 pp.67–9.

ning of the next chapter or episode. This device is often explained as the
storyteller's professional safeguard – at the peak of suspense, he circu-
lated among his clients to collect the fee.[1]

However, a quite thrilling expectation for the medieval listener or
reader was also aroused by the content and structure of the episodes.
Most *chu-kung-tiao* episodes tell how the hero's enemies or other obstacles keep him from his goal. In this manner the structure of the episode itself (obstacle-fight-victory) generates a tension for the medieval
receiver (Will the hero be able to pass the barriers or will he fail?),
postpones the final dénouement of the plot, and make it also more
complex and more attractive to the storyteller's audience. However,
the effect of the episodes which repeatedly tell about the challenges to
the hero can be explained not only as a rhetorical device – they also
stress to a great extent the dominant message of both *chu-kung-tiao*. In
the case of *Liu Chih-yüan chu-kung-tiao*, the episodes reinforce the idea,
already demonstrated by the character-type which Liu Chih-yüan represents: a man, once predestined to be an Emperor, becomes the ruler no
matter how many obstacles he encounters on his way to the throne. In
the case of *Hsi-hsiang chi chu-kung-tiao*, the message becomes even
stronger: because the fate of the lovers does not develop automatically
in their favour, they must make an enthusiastic effort to ensure their
eventual happy union.

As in *hsiao-shuo*[2], *chu-kung-tiao* is introduced by a short prologue
(*yin-tzu* 'introduction'), usually consisting of several lyric poems
loosely connected thematically with the main story and functioning
as a kind of story-teller's advertisement. The *yin-tzu* induced the proper
mood for the main subject and announced the theme of the story to
be performed. At the very end of the *Liu Chih-yüan chu-kung-tiao* performance, a short epilogue is inserted in which the story-teller lets his
audience know where the theme came from and announces that his
performance is finished.

VII

Many European romances in the Middle Ages were written in what
we may call a prosimetric form; one in which prose and verse alternate.

---

[1] It is quite interesting to observe how *Hsi-hsiang chi chu-kung-tiao* was divided
into chapters in different editions. In the two earliest editions, when *chu-kung-tiao*
was still closely connected with the story-teller's performance, chapters are divided
as indicated. However, in all later editions, after *chu-kung-tiao* became entertainment for readers, chapters concluded at places dictated by the logic of the events.
[2] Cf. C. Birch: 'Some Formal Characteristics of the *hua-pen* Story', BSOAS, 17
(1955), 346–64, esp. 348–50.

The best and most famous example is probably the French *chantefable* of the thirteenth century, *Aucassin et Nicolette*, but there are a number of other prosimetric creations in European literature which are somewhat less well known – Dante's *Vita Nuova*, Belleau's *Journée de la Bergerie*, and Sannazaro's *Arcadia*.

The source of this highly versatile and artistically powerful device may be Arab and Indian literature and it appears quite possible that prosimetric form was introduced into Chinese literature (most particularly to Chinese story-tellers' literature) from India during the era when Buddhist *sūtras* were being translated in China.

Though a certain number of Chinese story-tellers' compositions are written exclusively in either prose or verse, the majority of them incorporate both. In some forms – *hsiao-shuo* for example – verse appears only occasionally (often with a minimum relationship to the story), but in others verse becomes as important as prose, the two parts forming an indivisible whole.

While prose is the prime vehicle for advancing the story in *chu-kung-tiao*, the verse elaborates and dilates the simple epic line of prose by lyric descriptions. In contrast, prose sections seem almost atrophied; their language runs to verbs and nouns and is nearly telegraphic. The terseness of the prose also must have been exaggerated by the fact that it was narrated in a speaking voice while the verse was sung.

Contrary to the epic dynamism and stylistic sobriety of prose, verse in *chu-kung-tiao* brings the story to a halt momentarily, but it is always the most artistically effective part of the work. Just as the *chu-kung-tiao* composer overwhelms his simpler model with elaborations of his own, so his verse overshadows the prose by poetic imagination and individual creativity. Adjectives and intensifiers seem to be the most important linguistic vehicle in the verse sections and their aesthetic effect must have been hightened by being set to music.

The alternation and contrast between lean, sober prose and colourful, expansive verse worked to the benefit of each. The prose appears compact and dynamic in contrast to the sung verse and the songs gain appeal and richness when restrained by narrated prose. The composer also adds interest to his product by inserting occasional paired sayings (*tui-lien*) and quatrains of poetry which resemble older T'ang literary styles. Taken all together the genre represents a great advance in complexity and aesthetic potential over anything we know of from earlier times.

DRAMATIS PERSONAE

Liu Chih-yüan or *Hidden Dragon*, the emperor-to-be of the Han Dynasty

Li San-niang, his first wife

Ch'eng-yu, their son

Li San-chuan or *Li the Learned*, Liu Chih-yüan's father-in-law

Li San-weng, brother of Li San-chuan

Li Hung-hsin
Li Hung-i } Liu Chih-yüan's brothers-in-law

'Topsy-turvy'
'Prickle stick' } Liu Chih-yüan's sisters-in-law

Mu-jung Yen-ch'ao
Mu-jung Yen-chin } Liu Chih-yüan's half-brothers

Yüeh Ssu-kung, Brigade General and Liu Chih-yüan's second father-in-law

Lady Yüeh, General's daughter and Liu Chih-yüan's second wife

Li Hsin, General Yüeh's officer and go-between

Chapter the First

HOW CHIH-YÜAN LEFT THE MU FAMILY COMPOUND AND LIVED AS SON-IN-LAW AT SHA-T'O VILLAGE

∾∾∾∾∾∾∾∾∾∾∾∾∾∾∾∾∾∾∾∾∾∾∾∾∾∾∾∾∾∾∾

2a[1]   (Shang-tiao mode, *hui-ko-yüeh* melody)

Introduction

(*yin-tzu*)

Idly I read old books by my window,
I turn the leaves
Watching seventeen generations pass.
In ancient times and still today, the world was ever turbulent,
From Kung Kung's[2] fight at Pu-chou-shan and Ch'ih Yu's[3]
churning of the dust,
Through T'ang's attack on Chieh[4]
To king Wu's muster of troops to seize the lands of Chou.[5]

Wu and Yüeh destroyed themselves[6] and the seven states made war with one another.

[1] The marginal numbers refer to the pages of the photo-reprint ed. Peking, 1958.
[2] A demon who fought the legendary Emperor Chuan Hsü and broke the Pu-chou mountain, one of the eight pillars which hold up the sky, by butting into it.
[3] Usually spoken of as an unsuccessful rebel against Huang-ti, the mythical Yellow Emperor (2697–2597 B.C.), but also a demon.
[4] T'ang defeated Chieh, the last Emperor of the Hsia Dynasty and became the founder of the succeeding Shang Dynasty (1766–1122 B.C.).
[5] King Wu, founder of the Chou Dynasty (1122–255 B.C.), vanquished Chou, the infamous last ruler of the Shang Dynasty.
[6] Wu and Yüeh, two ancient kingdoms during the Ch'un-ch'iu period (722–480 B.C.). Wu in the delta of Yang-tze river and Yüeh on the south-east coast were inhabited by a people distinct from the Chinese.

Then gradually began the wars of Ch'u and Han.
Till, finally, Kao-tsu's latent powers equalled Heaven's own
And gave his state four hundred years of peace.
Midway through that age, a seditious man arose.
Wang Mang took the throne,
But Kuang-wu at the battle of K'un-yang
Swept all his work away.[1]

In the end, Three Kingdoms rose.[2]
Never once were arms and weapons put away.
Most tragic were dynasties of Chin[3] and Ch'en[4] and Sui.[5]
Often and again the smoke of signal fires ringed the land.
Through twenty-one rulers flourished mighty T'ang,
Till Hsi-tsung heeded slanderous words.
T'ang's throne lost its sway again.
Thereafter, rose Five Dynasties and all the worst of famine and of pain.[6]

---

[1] Han Dynasty brought about the unification of China which lasted four centuries (206 B.C.–A.D. 220). Its founder was Liu Pang, a humble peasant, whose imperial name was Kao-tsu. The throne was later 'usurped' by Wang-Mang. He was killed in the battle of K'ung-yang and a prince, who later became Emperor Kuang-wu (A.D. 25–57) founded the Later Han Dynasty.

[2] Three Kingdoms (San-kuo), namely Wei in the north, Wu in the east and the Shu-Han in the west reigned simultaneously in different parts of China during the third century A.D.

[3] Two Dynasties of Chin, namely Western Chin and Eastern Chin, ruled over China between A.D. 265 and A.D. 419.

[4] Between A.D. 420 and A.D. 589 China was divided among several dynasties which reigned in the north and south. This era in Chinese history is usually called the Period of Northern and Southern Dynasties. Using the rhetoric of *pars pro toto*, the author of the *chu-kung-tiao* mentions only the Ch'en Dynasty (557–87) instead of enumerating all of them.

[5] The Sui Dynasty reunited China, but it lasted only 29 years (A.D. 589–618).

[6] The T'ang Dynasty (618–906) was one of the most famous and powerful in China's history. During the Emperor Hsi-tsung's reign (874–89) Huang Ch'ao, the leader of a peasant rebellion, defeated the imperial army. The Emperor fled to his western capital in Szechuan province and Huang Ch'ao proclaimed himself Emperor. The ensuing era is usually called the Period of the Five Dynasties (907–60). Further in the text, the author of the *chu-kung-tiao* complains especially about two of these dynasties, Liang (907–23) and Chin (936–47).

da) Huang Ch'ao and his rebellion then appears
To distress the people even more
For fifty long chaotic years.

2b   How do we know that during the Five Dynasties disasters and dis-
turbance succeeded one another? An ancient sage once wrote the
following lines:

When Emperor Hsi-tsung's carriage escaped to the West,
His noblemen were all cast down, but humble men rose from the mud.
Hamlet elders all were officers of middle rank.
Officers' ladies became the wives of common men.
Dirty hands which held the plough, hold now the ceremonial plaque.
Red lips, used to eating meat, must be content with salted leeks.
One thing only could not be changed:
The southern clouds still float as high as Nan-shan's peaks.[1]

(Cheng-kung, *Ying-t'ien-ch'ang ch'an-ling*)

Since misery and wars began,
Never were so many battles fought as during Liang and Chin.
Famous men and wealthy now became the poor –
The poor grew rich and honoured.
In such a way chancellor became commoner
And common men could hold the highest post.

This tale tells of Ying-chou *lu*,[2]
Of two men and their mother who
Lived through many a hardship.
The older son was Liu Chih-yüan,
The younger's name was Liu Chih-ch'ung[3]

---

[1] *Nan-shan* peaks, the peaks of southern mountain ranges, a symbol of constancy.
[2] *Lu*, the largest administrative unit during the Sung period (960–1279) and the
second largest during the Yüan (1280–1368).
[3] Liu Chih-ch'ung, in the *chu-kung-tiao* is spoken of as Liu Chih-yüan's brother,
but he was actually his cousin and was called Liu Ch'ung. When Liu Chih-yüan's
dynasty collapsed in 950, he declared himself Emperor at Ping-chou. His dynasty
is known as the Pei Han or Tung Han (Northern or Eastern Han).

And each was the constant comrade of the other,
Though Chih-yüan had reached manhood when
Chih-ch'ung was only eight or nine – as yet a child –
Who thought as children think.

(Kan-ts'ao-tzu)

In their home, in their home,
All the elders had been statesmen.
Their father a famous soldier was,
Whose given name was Kuang-t'ing.
3a A battle he lost, in which he died.
And now because the family fortune's spent
They leave their home – south to friendlier soil.
Penniless and cold they went –
What misery, such toil!

(Coda) The rulers of two dynasties have found
The times were out of joint for them:
Chih-ch'ung destined to become
Emperor of all the land between the Yellow River and the sea.
Chih-yüan, the Hidden Dragon,[1] First Ancestor of the Han to be.

The *History of Five Dynasties* says: Kao-tsu of the Han dynasty was surnamed Liu, his given name was Chih-yüan. After he had become Emperor, he changed his given name to Kao. His ancestors were descended from the Sha-t'o.[2] His father's name was Kuang-t'ing and he died in battle. After this, the family fortune was dispersed and Chih-yüan together with his younger brother Chih-ch'ung followed their mother to find friendlier soil near T'ai-yüan. In Liu-pao village of the Yang-p'an district lived a man named Mu-jung whose given name was Ta-lang. He married their mother and took her as his second wife. She

[1] In ancient China, the dragon personified the Emperor. A 'Hidden Dragon' is an Emperor not yet enthroned.
[2] *Sha-t'o*, a Turkish tribal confederation during the Five Dynasties. Very few in number, probably little more than 100,000 men, it never gained significance in Chinese political life. Nevertheless, several famous generals (Li K'o-yung, Shih Chin-t'ang and Liu Chih-yüan) came from this confederation.

bore him two sons, namely Yen-ch'ao and Yen-chin. When they had
grown, her first two sons disliked their half-brothers. Chih-yüan alone
left the house and took himself to another place. Alas, he left without
a penny for his trip.

(Hsien-lü-tiao, *liu-yao-ling*)

Each day was like another,
On what day would his destined power show?
One morning, fortune will come
And then his fame will spread through China and barbarian lands.
But now he is the priceless jade from Ching-shan,
Still untouched by Pien Ho's hands.[1]
And just as the flood dragon can hide
In the shallow seep of a horse's hoofprint,
3b So his destiny awaits auspicious clouds and rainbow arcs.

He went his way lacking money,
So on the road he suffered trials and hunger.
While travelling he fixed his eyes [upon the distant view].
Suddenly saw a village and its fallow-land
Not three miles off.
His steps then seemed to make him fly.
Once there, he looked at all the farmsteads
With their fine fat fields.
Then coming nearer to the high road, he found a newly opened
inn,
With its signpole thrust aslant above its picket fence.

la) More impressive than a battle pennon above a border fort
The guild-flag of the wine-shop, three feet long,
Stirred in every breeze from where it hung.

---

[1] Pien Ho, a legendary connoisseur of jade, supposed to have lived some time
between the eighth and fifth centuries B.C. in the feudal state of Ch'u. He discovered the mountain Ching-shan to be a rich deposit of nefrite.

Scattered, thatched huts by the road,
The wine shop's flag above them all.
A cheerful fire in the stove.
This mud and ox-dung building showed
The Drunken Genius[1] on its wall.
The innkeeper's name was Buffalo Niu – seventh son of his family.
The Hidden Dragon entered the shop and greeted him.

(Hsien-lü-tiao, *sheng-hu-lu*)

Innkeeper Niu Ch'i-weng offered his wares.
Liu Chih-yüan looked cautiously about.
In this place none paid the king's tax nor any other. (?)
What matter if everyone here, this hundred years gone by,
Was sodden drunk each day?
That would still be somewhat less than
Thirty-six thousand drunks in all!
The bowls were of brown ware.
Porcelain tea-pots on brick benches all in rows.
The wine tastes better here than at Kao-yang –
No sooner is one bowl down than you seize its mate
To sip and suck and lick its slippery sides.
. . . .
[*fourth page missing*]

5a . . . his beard stuck out as though it were a brush;
His neck and chest were like the hide of a bear.

Ch'i-weng saw him and wrinkled up his brow.
'Listen carefully, my guest, to all I tell you now:
'This man is always for himself whatever he hopes others think,
'He'll snatch your bench to seat himself and nothing does he well
but drink.
'An uninvited guest, he is proper only in his appetite.

---

[1] The Drunken Genius usually refers to the great Chinese poet Li Po (A.D. 701–61).

'In the village he's the first to cheat the well-intended,
'Respect for others he knows as little of
'As humility with himself.
'When people see him, they flee him as they would a ghoul.
'He vexes all of us and nothing escapes his grasp.

da) 'The plague of this place is he.
'In the village no one calls him Li Hung-i,
'For here he's named the Living Vampire.'

> This man lived in Hsiao-li village of the Sha-t'o district. His family name was Li and his given name Hung-i. Because he was no good, they all called him Living Vampire. Liu should have avoided him. But suddenly Hung-i burst into the wineshop and hurled a string of insults at Ch'i-weng. When the Hidden Dragon had heard enough of it, he flushed in anger. He wished to repay the innkeeper who had been kind enough to give him a meal.

(Nan-lü-kung, *yao-t'ai-yüeh*)

He behaved as would the crudest oaf,
Treating that old man
As though he were so much refuse.
He shouted
And commanded him like a slave
And bullied the poor old one until he feared to raise his head.
He asked what Hung-i wished and being told could only say
'Yes, yes.'
5b He served Hung-i his best wine.
But otherwise dared not move a step.
When Ch'i-weng saw Hung-i's
Eyebrows go up and down,
He was stiff with fear.

When he saw Hung-i happy and laughing, he knew relief and laughed excessively.

When his guest showed a sign of distaste, he furrowed his brow.
Still insults of every sort continued
Till Chih-yüan, sitting to one side, flew into a towering rage.
And roared aloud like a clap of spring thunder.
He still hoped to repay the old man's kindness – for he had given
him food to eat –
He shouted: 'You, you lout, listen to me!
'Uneducated you may be,
'But even you can figure out,
'Who is great and who is small
'And learn from others, how to act toward all.

(Coda) 'A hulking fellow as old as you
'Should never revile a person so.
'Think of your own parents
'And wonder, you dog, how you treated them long ago!

   'I wonder, have you never heard the proverb: "When there are old
people in the family, one must cherish them. When there are cows and
sheep on the farm, you must respect the grass in the meadow?" Among
the five fortunes,[1] high age is the most admirable. Judging by your
bad manners, you are no more than a beast.' Hung-i flew into a fury.

(P'an-she-tiao, *ch'iang-t'ou-hua*)

The innkeeper was so frightened
He almost lost his wits.
'My boy', he thought, 'you have courage enough.
'But you don't know this ruffian
'Or you'd not want to curse and fight him.'

With good intent he urged them both be calm.
But more and more, the fury grew upon their brows,

---

[1] The five fortunes: longevity, wealth, health, virtue, and to finish one's allot-
ted span.

And soon it was apparent that this day his shop would be demolished.

The proverb says: 'When two hard things meet head on.
6a One of them will surely be destroyed.'

The oaf struck out with his fist,
But Liu Chih-yüan was very cool.
He stepped aside, slid past the blow,
He clenched his fist and balled it tight
As a chestnut. Then with all his might
He smote him with the 'ox-felling blow' from the other side.

da) Hung-i could not remain upright.
His face was beaten and his nose was smashed.
Straight down upon the hardwood table top he crashed.

Chih-yüan's impetus was like a dragon
Surging from the uprushing waves.
The bully's weakness
Was like a mortally wounded tiger with indrawn claws.
Poor Li Hung-i, the nobleman-to-be, had lost to the Emperor, whose name was not yet known. Hung-i was badly hurt and Niu Ch'i-weng begged them both to stop. All the men in the tavern cheered. And a moment later, off went the Living Vampire.

(Cheng-kung, *wen-hsü-tzu*)

He saved his life by the width of a needle, dare he stay a moment more?
Blood flowed from every place, his bones were bruised, his flesh was scratched.
He was the wild tiger which sheathes its teeth and claws, its spirit broken.
Always he had been the best of all at kicking and boxing,
A perfect ruffian.

But Heaven had brought calamity to youth and ill fortune to a bully.

6b Ashamed, he could not raise his head nor look another in the eye.
Straightway he ran out the wine-shop door and stammered:
'All right, all right!
But I'll never let you off!'

(Coda) Enemies are tied together like a river and a sea.
In the future, this villager will be
The Hidden Dragon's mortal foe.

When Chih-yüan heard the threat, he made no great matter of it, but passed the night at Niu Ch'i-weng's shop. The next day, he said good-bye to the innkeeper and wandered from one village to the next, drifting as would fallen flower petals or poplar-cotton curls.

(Hsieh-chih-tiao, *chen-p'ing-erh*)

The Hidden Dragon, whose time had not yet come,
Passed the night in a wine-shop.
When the day was breaking, he bade good-bye to Ch'i-weng
To set out once again across the land.
But when he thought about his future
He felt more and more in doubt.
For after all where could he go?

Wending and winding was the road as he set out
And it was just the first of Spring.
Willow fluff dancing in the wind, falling petals flying in the air,
Orioles chasing butterflies winging slowly past.
Suddenly he is close to a village.
The elms and sophoras touch one another with their branches.
In the shadow of the trees he rested for a time.

You could only see scattered cow-sheds at the rear of the farmyard

and simple houses facing South. Hemp was spread on the tender green
7a grass and the *yeh-ku*[1] shone amidst the moss. Tired Chih-yüan slept.
In the sophora shadow he slept so deeply he knew nothing. From the
compound an old man came, leaning upon a bamboo stick, and when
he reached the trees, he saw beneath them the man sleeping on the
ground.

(Shang-chiao, *ting-feng-p'o*)

Then came the old one out of the compound.
I suppose he was the most respected man in all his clan.
Most orderly his clothes and well made up:
In his hand he held a bamboo staff.
Into the fields he went
Away from the village for half a mile perhaps,
Where wind blew the grain in waves as far as the eye could see.

Suddenly, he is startled;
In the sophora shadow he sees a purple mist, a crimson glow,
Before his eyes a golden dragon plays with a priceless pearl.
And still the vision lingers and covers the Emperor,
Who lay sound asleep and snored like thunder.
While about his face shone all the auspices of kingship.

da) The old man, moved, sighed for what the future would bring.
Within the hour, this homeless man would doubtless leave
Yet far in the future this Hidden Dragon would be king.

The old man said with a sigh: 'One day this man will certainly be
honoured though I have not yet got what manner of honour it will
be.' He waited for a while and the youth awoke. Whereupon the old
one asked him his name and native place, for he hoped to make a
friend of him. Chih-yüan answered him.

---

[1] *Yĕh-kŭ* 野 鼓, 'wild drums' should probably be *yĕh-kū* 野 菰, *Aeginatia indica*.

(Shang-tiao, *p'ao-ch'iu-lo*)

7b The old man inquired
And the Hidden Dragon could not refuse him.
He longed to speak of his hardships,
He brooded on his misfortunes once again –
A stream of tears flowed down his cheek.
Then he sobbed and finally
Clasped his hands and began to speak
'I want to tell you my life story.
'But I am so poor I wear only a hempen singlet,
'Who will believe me if I speak of honoured ancestors?
'Yet once our family fame and heritage were glorious.
'For centuries my forebears served constantly at court.
'My father died in the battle ranks
'And when the end of T'ang had come
'And chaos raised the frontier battle beacons,
'My mother took my younger brother and me
'And all of us left our native place.

'Haggard and hungry – suffering, shivering,
'How do men survive starvation and cold?
'In Yang-p'an village we met a good man
'Who asked my mother to be his wife.
'She bore him two sons. But when they'd grown,
'They proved worthless.
'Chin-erh and Chao-erh are their names.
'They lent their ears to gossip
'And quarrelled with me angrily over what they heard.
'Always, we were at each others' throats.
'They mocked me for my surname was not theirs.
'Should a full-grown man bear taunts from children?
'Sore at heart I left my home,
'And though I know not how, my legs
'Have brought me to your compound.
'Where you, good sir, have been so courteous.'

oda) Once they lived in Ying-chou, in the district of Chin-ch'eng,
But savage wars and chaos stole their land away.
Now, even to speak his family name
Pains him deeply, pricks his shame.
Poor, homeless Liu Chih-yüan who begs his food each day.

8a   When the old man heard his words, he asked him once again: 'If
you dislike being poor and without a family, I own many fields in this
village, but I have few labourers. Won't you work for me, so we may
help each other for six months or a year?' Chih-yüan went with him
and when they had entered the village, they asked one Wang, the
scribe, to write them up a contract.

(Cheng-kung, *chin-ch'an-tao*)

Well, imagine now:
The Emperor-to-be, Hidden Dragon,
Has no choice.
He must wend and wind and wander from one village
To the next and beg his meals.
By chance, he comes to Hsiao-li-ts'un of the Sha-t'o
And tells an old man the story of his life.
And both agree
To have a contract written.
'When a half year is over, we'll talk about it more . . .
'I'll make it even better: I'll throw in clothes and meals.'

And so it happened that
Liu Chih-yüan came to the old man's home.
But in the main hall of the house
Two old women made wry faces.
The older quickly called her spouse.
Liu Chih-yüan peered to see him
And suddenly was startled.
'Why, he's the one in the wine-shop yesterday
Who ordered food and drink.
The one I nearly kicked apart and clouted silly!'

(Coda) Mortal enemies have met before in lives gone by:
It was no other than his enemy, Li Hung-i.
Predestined trouble no one can deny!

8b   Li Hung-i recognized his rival also. He seized a stick and rushed
forward to beat Liu Chih-yüan. What now of the Hidden Dragon's
life? (Repetition.)[1] The old man's family name was Li and he was
the oldest in his clan. Because he knew so much of days gone by and
was familiar with books and geomancy, people called him San-chuan
– The Learned. His two sons were worthless. The elder's name was
Li Hung-i, the younger was called Hung-hsin. Both their wives had
nicknames: the elder's wife was the kind who could climb a tree feet
first if she had to – a 'Topsy-turvy'; the younger was called 'Prickle-
stick'. When they saw Liu Chih-yüan, they made unhappy faces. The
elder of the brothers, Li Hung-i, wanted to beat him, but Li, the
Learned stopped him saying: 'This man signed a contract to work for
me. My son, why should you be so angry with a handyman?'

(Huang-chung-kung, *yüan-ch'eng-shuang*)

Li the Learned frowned and said:
'Why, my son, are you so mad?'
Then said he, pointing to the new come youth:
'He is from a rich and famous clan.

'He suffers, because his father died in battle
'And his mother married once again.
'Forlorn, alone, he wandered through the land
'And now will work for us for wages.

(Coda) 'Are you so doltish and coarse of grain
'That you would drive the stranger out?
'You raise that stick just once again
'And we will see who gets a clout!'

---

[1] We imagine that this cryptic note, '*yün-yün*', meant that the story-teller
recapitulated the tale here in some way.

9a   Hung-i did not tell his father about the earlier fight in the wine-shop, saying only that he did not like the man.

Because they had not yet paid their district taxes and levies, both brothers had to leave to see to it. 'But when we get back, he'd better not be here.' Saying these words, they saddled their horses and left. The old man did not worry about it but lodged Liu Chih-yüan in the western building. Li's daughter was called San-niang and when she burned incense that evening, she saw a golden snake several inches long in the moonlight which crawled towards the western chamber.

(Chung-lü-tiao, *an-kung-tzu ch'an-ling*)

She was just a country maid,
Yet beautiful beyond compare.
Not Lo-fu, Hsi-shih, nor Ta-chi[1]
Had ever been as beautiful as she.
She was fifteen, just the age when girls begin to dress their hair
And she as yet was not betrothed.
Willow-leaf brows, skin of the peach, and a cherry mouth.
Her flesh was transparent jade, her waist slender
And she knew how to walk in her golden-lotus shoes.

Everything she wore fit handsomely
And her silk clothes were touched with golden threads.
Each evening it was her wont to burn
Incense to the bright, pale moon:
This night she was frightened.
For on the floor, in a shaft of golden light
She clearly saw a little snake, seven inches long,
Go straight to the western hall
The door of which was left ajar.

---

[1] Lo-p'u, Hsi-shih, and Ta-chi, three famous Chinese beauties. Lo-p'u, probably Lo-fu, famous heroine of the ballad 'Mulberries on the Dykes', often called 'The Song of Lo-fu'. Hsi-shih traditionally lived during the fifth century B.C. and her loveliness caused the defeat of the Prince of Wu, her master. Ta-chi was the favourite of the last ruler of the Shang Dynasty (twelfth century B.C.).

(Liu-ch'ing-niang)

This lovely girl went swiftly to the room
9b Where on the wall a lamp was dimly winking.
With a golden pin she raised the wick
And brought the light up blazing bright.
On an earthen bed there lay a youth
Seven feet tall and fair of face.
His imperial body was awesome as a god's,
His eyes were closed and he soundly slept.
Never had San-niang witnessed such a thing.

(Su-tsao-erh)

Red glow and violet mist covered his body,
And the aura showed his good fortune was inexhaustible.
The little snake wriggled in and out his nostrils.
San-niang was delighted:

(Liu-ch'ing-niang)[1]

'Once a soothsayer said that I'd know fame,
'That I would become an Emperor's wife,
'That I would be Empress and marry a noble man.
'Surely this night bears out the prophet's words.
'In these last days of the house of T'ang
'Some cannot tell the Imperial Dragon from a common snake,
'But an Emperor-to-be has found our compound good
'So I must straightway pay him my respects.

(Coda) ' "Who cannot recognize a pearl remains poor."
'If I reject the auspicious sign
'Will Chao-yang palace[2] ever be mine?'

---

[1] This is the longest *t'ao-shu* (suite) in the whole work: four separate tunes and a coda before the mode changes.

[2] Chao-yang Palace, literally Bright and Shining Palace, traditionally belonged to the Empress.

Thereupon San-niang took the ornamented silver pin from her hair and broke it in half. When the Hidden Dragon awoke, with both hands she passed it to him. When he saw San-niang in the light of her lamp, he was startled and said: 'I am a poor man and grateful to your ba father who was kind to me. But I am a hired hand on your farm, so leave here quickly, please. If your brothers and their wives knew you were here I would surely be in trouble.' San-niang replied with smile: 'Sir, you need not be afraid, I come a-purpose to make your acquaintance.'

(Huang-chung-kung, *nü-kuan-tzu*)

Then the Hidden Dragon knew surprise,
Quickly he leaped from his earthen bed.
Politely he bowed and asked:
'What is the reason, Madam,
'You come here deep in the night?
'Please, leave the western chamber soon,
'It were better for me if you did,
'For if the old one knew of it
'I would surely be in trouble.'

San-niang was unabashed.
'I came to present myself to the Emperor', said she.
'I look toward the time when he will live
'In palaces and wander through royal parks.'
Then in a low voice she said to him:
'Sir, fear nothing.
'The day I saw you come to our compound
'I knew you were no mean or common man.
'First, let us announce our betrothal
'And then we'll wed.'
Then breaking her silver pin
She gave one half to Liu Chih-yüan.

da) 'Though we are not wed, let me share my pin with you.
When you are Emperor we'll live together as man and wife.

As Princess Yüeh-ch'ang did with Hsü Te-yen,[1]
Let me pledge to you my life.'

Liu Chih-yüan could not refuse the pin but other than this nothing
passed between them. The next day, San-niang told her father privately
that in the night, she had seen a golden snake crawling through Liu
Chih-yüan's nostrils. The old man was very happy.

10b   (Nan-lü kung, *ying-t'ien-ch'ang*)

Little San-niang cared nothing for what the family might say.
Behind her sister-in-law's back
She gave one pin from her pair in token of her faith.
Early next day, she visited her parents
And told them again what had happened in the night.
'Yesterday I burned incense
'In the western hall. My eyes were quickly caught
'By a snake, whose golden gleam shone bright,
'Which crawled here and there and wound about.

'Till it came by chance upon the youthful stranger
'And knowing him, crawled straight into his nose.
'In spite of that the stranger did not move.
'Father please, explain to me
'This matter I find so strange.'
When he heard her tale, the old man said:
'He is a youth whose name is Liu.
'He will, we know not when, be honoured beyond any doubt.

[1] There is a legend about the Princess Yüeh-ch'ang, the younger sister of the Emperor Hou-chu from the Ch'en Dynasty (557–589), and her husband Hsü Te-yen.
The territory of Ch'en being surrounded by the army of Sui Dynasty, Hsü
Te-yen had to do to battle and leave his wife. The princess broke a bronze mirror,
gave half to her husband and told him to go the 15th day of the first lunar month
to the market in the capital. If he found her half which she would keep until
market day and then sell, she would be somewhere nearby. The Ch'en Dynasty
perished and the two were separated for a long time. But on the fixed day, Hsü
Te-yen went to the market, found his wife's half of the mirror, finally found
Princess Yüeh-ch'ang and they lived in love until death.

a) 'Once, my child, the fortune-teller said
'Our family's fate and fortune soon would change.
'And you would wear the Empress' cap upon your head.'

San-niang could not disobey her father so they spoke to the youth
and took him as a son-in-law. The beauty smiled, her mother, too,
was not opposed. Thereupon they inquired of San-weng, the third
oldest in the clan and he was also in accord. No one asked the opinion
of San-niang's brothers and their wives. San-weng was made the go-
between and asked a fortune-teller to choose an auspicious day.

1a   (Huang-chung-kung, *k'uai-huo-nien*)

Father and mother frowned no more.
San-weng gave his quick consent
And smiles of pleasure creased his cheeks.
But the brothers' wives both stood apart,
Their lips crooked sourly, taking no pleasure at all.
So very happy was San-niang, she could scarce contain herself.

But the trouble came with Li-Hung-i and Li Hung-hsin
Who seethed with evil rage
And all the while kept hatching plots,
For they were men of evil hearts:
'Our mortal foe!'
'How can we take him into our home?' they asked,
And so saying sent a servant on ahead
To tell [their feelings to the clan].

da) 'When happiness is at its peak, bad luck is near to hand.'
So this new joy was doomed to die,
When the servant brought her brothers' command.

They jumped from their horses, strode into the compound and
hearing talk of the wedding wished to prevent it. But before they
could, Li the Learned, and San-weng said: 'One day Mr. Liu will be
famous and your fortune will improve too.'

(Hsien-lü tiao, *liu-yao-ling*)

Hung-hsin and Hung-i,
Angry still and far from mollified
Would not stop but nursed the anger in their hearts.
Time and again they shot a glance at Liu Chih-yüan
Which showed their resolve to get revenge another day.
'You have married into our house
'So we are now your kin,
11b 'But one day we'll forget ourselves
'And give you a good drubbing down!'

San-weng, sitting in the seat of honour,
Heard and shouted angrily:
'You idiots, you fools,
'To insult this man so recklessly!
'Today our guest is no one,
'A Dragon, sick, with indrawn teeth and claws,
'But soon a storm will come
'To blow him wealth and fame
'And through him you will know honour too.

(Coda) 'Your door will show the sign to exempt you from *corvée*,
'Cord sandals will become silken boots!
'Court robes of violet silk, not cotton gowns each day.'

The family heeded neither Hung-hsin nor Hung-i, but chose a fortunate day and hour for the wedding and asked their relatives to come. They milled the flour, prepared the wine, and arranged the bridal feast. When evening came, the two were wed.

(Shang-tiao, *yü-pao-tu*)

All the many relatives, smiling,
Watched for San-niang's manner
And Chih-yüan's mien and found
Husband and wife well matched indeed.

When San-niang's eyes glanced sidewise, autumn waters leaped.
When Chih-yüan's brows were moved, a line of clouds grew
dense.
They were as two trees with twining branch
Or *pi-yi* birds dependent on each other's wing.[1]
They were the phoenix and its mate in their marriage harmony.
They were beyond compare, pre-eminent,
And all the villagers rejoiced.
Only Hung-hsin and Hung-i
(With both their wives) nursed a sullen rage.

Those two oafs were in their cups,
All groggy, muzzy, red of face.
They boxed and kicked and shrieked and screeched,
Confusing guest with friend,
Till everything went out of harmony.
Still, it was like a lively scene
From the 'Picture of Yao's People'.[2]
At the hour when cattle and sheep return to the fold
Li San-weng, heeding the geomancer's words
Arranged the marriage bed to face south-east.
The fortune-teller had said:
'This way their house will know no harm.'

Compared to a palace chamber it was a pauper's room,
But thatch hut must serve as imperial palace
For the future Empress bride and the Hidden Dragon groom.

That night the 'glow of good luck' veiled their poor dwelling, an
aura of happy fortune covered their round cottage of reeds. The
Emperor and Empress-to-be happily performed the rites of marriage

---

[1] *Pi-yi* birds have only one wing each and so can fly only in pairs.
[2] Yao, a mythical Emperor, traditionally reigned 2357–2255 B.C. Legend has it
that under his reign people were happy and joyful. Probably this legend was also
depicted by pictures, as mentioned in the text. There is a commonly used *ch'ü* by
the title of 'Yao's People' found in some fifty dramas.

and became husband and wife. The evening promised a century of
bliss, that night foretold their lifelong love. You two, husband and
wife, are as fish and water. But there were four people whose hearts
and natures were evil. The proverb says: 'When joy is at its peak,
disaster comes.' Hardly a hundred days after Chih-yüan's arrival in the
family as a son-in-law, his wife's father and mother both died. According to the ritual they dressed and fixed their hair in mourning. And
now three times seven days have passed since they buried their parents
and mourned them. Before, the brothers had been no good and their
wives made mischief, but now Li Hung-i and Li Hung-hsin became
unbridled.

12b   (P'an-she-tiao, *shua-hai-erh*)

Just three times seven days
Past the death of her father and mother,
And before the earth on their grave was dry,
Rude brother Hung-hsin and bad Hung-i let slip their rage.
They plotted to injure Liu Chih-yüan –
Aided by two envious women
Pouring venomous mischief in their ears,
All eager to insult Chih-yüan and hurt his wife.

When any mouth was opened it called Chih-yüan a pauper.
Each ordered him to attend them by the front steps.
There Hung-i cried out to his brother-in-law:
'Now hear me while I make things clear!
'Since you have been accepted in our family
'And you have settled in the village
'You'll learn to farm with me all day every day.
'You came to us with hands clasped for begging,
'A cuckoo in our nest who was capable of nothing!

(Coda) 'You dress yourself in fancy silken garments.
        'You neither dig the fields nor guide the ox nor plough.
        'You tell me, why should we suffer you in our compound now?'

Hung-i raised his club, stretched out his arm, and siezed Liu Chih-yüan by his clothes.

End of Chapter the First
HOW CHIH-YÜAN LEFT THE MU FAMILY COMPOUND AND LIVED AS SON-IN-LAW AT SHA-T'O VILLAGE

Chapter the Second

HOW LIU CHIH-YÜAN BADE SAN-NIANG GOOD-BYE AND JOINED THE ARMY IN T'AI-YÜAN

~~~~~~

Li Hung-i ripped Chih-yüan's fine clothes to rags and gave him a cotton gown and trousers to wear. Then he ordered him to tend the peach orchard. The Hidden Dragon did not know it was a plot and that the big fellow already waited for him in a dark place.

(Chung-lü-tiao, *mu-yang-kuan*)

The clouds came restlessly and went
Only a little rising moon appeared.
Unguessably wicked were Hung-hsin's plans.
He waited there for Liu Chih-yüan
As slowly the hour deepened into late night.
A short time after the watchman's second drum
A fresh wind blew upon men's cheeks.

The wall was tumbled on the north-west side
And suddenly, there, appeared another hero.
He leaped the ruined wall as nimble as could be
And poised to run to the thatched hut.
Hung-i was delighted.
The fellow was fit for death.
And all his grievances would be avenged!

1a) 'No man has a rear-looking eye to see his danger through.'
Li Hung-i cannot restrain his rage.
He will smite with his club his enemy's back
And break him quite in two.

2b
      Hung-i in rage
        Gripped the stick so tight it gave a puff of smoke.
      A man of stone
        Would be felled by such a stroke.
Struck such a blow on the back, the man was helpless. All seven
feet of him toppled to the earth with a heavy crash!

(Hsien-lü-tiao, *tsui-lo-t'o*)

Hung-i with an angry curse
Put all his strength into his hands.
Down fell the other, his heart full of hate,
Wishing he were dead, so great the pain.

Hung-i stooped, dragged the stranger up and looked at him.
In the light of the moon, he recognized the face.
It *wasn't* the pauper Liu Chih-yüan,
He looked more carefully – it was Li Hung-hsin!

    Hung-i between fright and smile, Hung-hsin between pain and
patience. 'I was afraid that you, big brother, would not be able to down
that paupered devil. That's why I came to watch you.' It has been true
from the beginning of time that the net of Heaven stretches everywhere. Its meshes are wide, but nothing escapes it. In a moment, they
saw Chih-yüan followed by several men. They all came smelling of
wine. Hung-i grabbed him: 'Our father and mother are dead but a
few days. How dare you drink!' The villagers replied: 'We only drink
to keep from crying.' But the brothers would not let be. When morning
came, they bound Liu Chih-yüan with rope and would have taken
him to court, but San-weng got wind of it.

3a   (Huang-chung-kung, *shuang-sheng tieh-yün*)

Li Hung-hsin and Li Hung-i
Bound the Hidden Dragon
And together began an endless din:
'Since he came to our home as a son-in-law
'He's looked upon us as children's toys.
'We'd say go this way and he'd go that!
'Always wrangling!

'We told him to mind the orchard, uncle,
'And back he came soggy drunk.
'We clouted him and he got mad
'And picked a fight with us!
'Uncle, judge who is right and who is wrong.'
When San-weng heard their words,
He shouted angrily: 'Quiet, you cattle!

(Coda) 'You both pick on him whenever you can
'Yet now complain *he's* mannerless –
'Well, which of *you* is a gentleman?'

   'If you take him to court', said San-weng, 'I'll fix you before the
judge!' Bystanders threatened him too, so Hung-i gave up. Several
days passed and the brothers laid another plot. They sent Liu Chih-yüan
to sleep in the thatched stable saying they thought the cow would soon
calve. Even San-niang was unaware of their plot and Chih-yüan did
not suspect them. When the deep of night had come, he slept soundly
inside the stable.

3b   (Nan-lü-kung, *ying-t'ien-ch'ang*)

Chih-yüan was depressed and sad at heart,
His tears flowed like rain.
Time and again he sighed at length

And secretly, he thought:
'Here am I, Ancestor-to-be [of the Han Dynasty]
'Born to a prominent family.
'We lost our wealth,
'I left my mother and all my kin,
'Heaven led me to this place.
'My father-in-law was very kind,
'He asked me to marrry his daughter
'And was happy he could help.

'My wife and I are the fish and the stream.
'Her parents we never did resent.
'But alas! Disaster! They both died.
'Li Hung-hsin and Li Hung-i have
'Nursed their hatred and harshly treated me.
'San-weng is fond of me and guards me from much harm
'But surely one day I'll be caught up by their plots.

da) 'My troubles riddle as hard as the *Classic of Filial Piety*![1]
'I love my San-niang; I wish to leave but cannot.
'Yet if I stay, can I bear our lot?'

> Held by San-niang's love
> He will grow old but never leave her.
> Thinking of the hatred of those two
> He cannot leave here fast enough.

4a   No way out has he. When will his sorrows cease? Late at night the
Hidden Dragon fell asleep. Outside the door, Li Hung-i listened
cautiously and his heart grew cruel as he began his wicked work.

---

[1] According to tradition, *Hsiao-ching*, the *Canon of Filial Piety*, was compiled on
the basis of the conversations between Confucius and his disciple Tseng-tzu. One
wonders why this should be used to describe a knotty problem.

(P'an-she-tiao, *ma-p'o-tzu*)

Hung-i judged it had passed the second watch.
The bright moon [sparkled] like an autumn river.
[Hung-i] approached so silently
One could have heard a light pin drop.
For a while he sat by the cow-pen,
Long he stayed and cocked his ear but finally was pleased.

He remembered: 'In the wine-shop . . .
'O, how I was knocked about!
'And then he was brought
'Into the family as a son-in-law –
'My father himself protected him!
'But now, how can he escape!
'He soundly sleeps, his snore is thunderlike.
'This thorn in my eye will soon be plucked out
'And after today I shall be glad again.'

(Coda) He's got him in a cow-shed covered with thick thatch.
To burn it down is simple,
Just bar the gate, toss the torch, and let the fire catch!

P'ang Chüan[1] himself was not as cruel
As this rustic wolf.
Huang Ch'ao[2] is merciful as Buddha
Compared to Hung-i.
Alas! The Emperor-to-be
Must end his life in the flames.

(Shang-chiao, *ting-feng-p'o*)

4b Liu Chih-yüan sleeps soundly and wakes not,
Snoring as the tigers roar amidst the hills.

[1] P'ang Chüan, envious, perfidious, and cruel general from the state of Wei during the period of the Warring States (403–221 B.C.).
[2] Huang Ch'ao, the leader of peasant's rebellion during the end of T'ang Dynasty. He perished in A.D. 884.

How can San-niang know
She may never meet her love again!
This is not pretend and not a dream,
His shade is destined to return to the Yellow Springs![1]

Just then Li Hung-i
Cups his ear and listens carefully.
He hesitates, he vacillates,
(Still, how can Chih-yüan save himself?)
And then as he touches torch to hut,
Suddenly a noise is heard that startles the great oaf.
He quickly jerks his head to look:

da) The stars have moved, the dipper's turned
And then it was third watch again.
Now will the Emperor's fortune show itself!
Clouds there were not nor even fog
Yet of a sudden it began to rain!

His sufferings were the same as Kuang Wu's.[2] His escape as miraculous as Chin Wang's[3] The rain quenched the fire. Chih-yüan awoke and though he knew Hung-i had done it, he dared not complain. Next day Chih-yüan harnessed the ox and donkey to their cart to work near the Temple of Three Religions. At noon, he rested for a while in the temple and slept. Soon a group of older villagers came there for respite from the summer heat. Li San-weng was among them.

---

[1] Yellow Springs, the Chinese Hades.

[2] After a violent civil war, the Emperor Kuang-wu regained the throne for the Han Dynasty (A.D. 25).

[3] Chin Wen-kung (the duke Wen of Chin) whose name was Ch'ung-erh, lived in the seventh century B.C. during the Ch'un-ch'iu era.

(P'an-she-tiao, *ch'in-yüan-ch'un*)

Liu Chih-yüan tied both ox and ass,
He did not think about the cart
But climbed the temple steps.
So troubled was he these many days past
5a He threw himself down in a heap
To sleep for a little while.
San-weng was standing by
And looked upon him anxiously,
His brows were knit.
'Here is a plight to wound the heart:
'Just this. A beautiful jade from Ching-shan hill
'Buried here deep in the mud!'

As the old man stood there saddened
Suddenly was heard a clap of thunder from the sky
And all were startled by the crash.
Then they saw the lightning flash
And it frightened them to death
It shook their souls out till none was left.
Then something caught their eyes
And they raised their heads to look:
In such a wild ill-omened storm [?]
The tender grain is battered down
And everywhere there'll be a desert
And famine-stricken folk.

(Coda) The good Dragon of the clouds
Has sent his devils with this rain.
Black clouds stretched across the skies
To pour the Four Seas down again.

The lightning darted silver snakes. The thunder pealed an iron gong, the winds dashed against the sky and the heavy rain was a torrent. The ox and donkey, frightened, snapped the hemp rope, ran away and disappeared to who knows where. San-weng shouted a warning to Chih-yüan who raced to catch the beasts, but they had gone. When it grew dark, Liu Chih-yüan did not dare return to the village.

(Kao-p'ing-tiao, *ho-hsin-lang*)

When Chih-yüan heard [San-weng's] shout, he jumped,
Left San-weng, and hurried from the shrine.
5b He cared not that his leather shoes got soiled
But searched all through the lake of mud.
Along the way he murmured to himself a thousand times:
'These two sons of piebald donkeys
'Will tie me to the mulberry tree
'And straightway I'll get fifty stripes.'

Now, history has come to the end of T'ang
And reached the age of Five Dynasties.
The people have lost their way; the multitudes are sore oppressed
But rich and famous men show bravery and brilliance.
And new-come heroes are hard and firm,
In T'ai-yüan district they brand their young recruits.
Chih-yüan wants to join but still he vacillates.
Not that he is of two minds
But is it strange that he should be pulled two ways at once?
So sad, so hard it is to leave San-niang!

When evening came, Liu Chih-yüan dared not return to the village. He wished to steal secretly away and join the army in T'ai-yüan. But his affection for San-niang is great; he cannot leave her. Under the bright moon, he could find neither sufficient reason for going or staying and he sighed again and again.

(Tao-kung, *chieh-hung*)

Wringing his hands and rubbing his fingers
Chih-yüan beneath the moon
Heaved a deep sigh and talked to himself:

'Could I have avoided kicking and boxing?
'Even no trouble at all causes trouble between Hung-i and me,
'Each of us irks the other so.
'How much worse it will be now,
'For I have lost both ox and ass!
'If I return to the village, what will they say?
'I am afraid to face Hung-hsin and Hung-i.
'I urge you, all young men and youths
'Try as best you can with each of your lives
'To avoid becoming a son-in-law such as I.

'While her parents were yet alive
6a 'All things were good and living easy.
'Since their death the others have harried my wife and me.
'Those men and their wives are never still,
'They find fault with everything in us.
'You can ruin any good man by slicing away at him
'Till he struggles for his very breath.
'I was so long poor, and not once rich
'They said that this could never change.
'Just a beggar owning nothing but a hearty appetite.
'Can a man stand five score insults such as these?
'Can anything good ever be cut from such cloth?'

(Coda) 'Throughout the village, grown men and young girls too
'Gave me a nickname, will they never stop?
'Everyone calls me Beggar Liu.'

　　It was slightly past the second watch, when Liu Chih-yüan secretly
returned. He had come to bid San-niang good-bye.

(Hsien-lü-tiao, *sheng-hu-lu*)

Beneath the moon moved Mr. Liu like a wisp of smoke,
His mouth still full of complaints
Because he hadn't found the ox and ass.

Holding back his alarm, containing his fear,
He tiptoed forward and travelled
Roundabout through the orchard.

'I say good-bye to my San-niang;
'I go to T'ai-yüan.
'When I'm in and branded
'We'll be together again.
'I walk but know not if I move little or much.
'So strong are the feelings of husband and wife
'This is like leaping a fence or scaling a wall
'While tied by a rope to one leg.'

6b
(da) Just then he approached the cattle-shed
To slip from sight, but slip he could not
For someone grabbed him by the arms instead.

    It frightened the Hidden Dragon to death. Who has seized him? He
turned his head – it was his wife San-niang. 'Husband, why do you
come so late? My brothers and their wives with clubs lie in wait for
you.' Chih-yüan told her the whys and the wherefores. 'Tonight, I
came just to say good-bye secretly, for I couldn't come openly to see
you.'

(Cheng-kung, chin-mo-tao)

Startled he turned in fear
And saw it was San-niang who caught him.
'I tell you, my husband,
'The work was hard enough before
'But after you left this morning
'I could hardly wait for dark.
'Oh, how anxious I grew!
'There was still no trace of you
'And my brothers and their wives were in such a rage!
'They're waiting for you now and will give you no quarter.'

What emotion!
As Chih-yüan listened to San-niang's words
His tears flowed like a spring.
He replied: 'In the temple of Three Religions,
'I hid myself to escape the heat.
'When I had fallen fast asleep
'It began to rain as though a cistern had overturned.
'When I awoke neither ox nor ass could be found
'And half the slope had turned into a lake.
'I searched for the beasts till evening came;
'In the dark of night I could not come through the main gate,
'So I leaped the wall to see my bride.

7a
(Coda) 'It will be hard to live in Sha-t'o-ts'un
'But stay, bear with your troubles, and farm the land.
'For I must go to Ping-chou ¹and take a soldier's brand.'

Dripping tears San-niang replied: 'If you go to T'ai-yüan, how will I get through the days?' Chih-yüan replied: 'The *an-fu* of nine districts² is raising an army now and I go to join it. I came here only to say good-bye.' When San-niang heard this, she felt a knife in her heart. 'I am already several months with child. I had to tell you.'

(Chung-lü-tiao, *mu-ta-sui*)

Li San-niang's black eyebrows knit,
She covered her sad face with cupped hands.
Then her delicate fingers caught Liu Chih-yüan's ragged clothes:
'If you go to T'ai-yüan to take the soldiers' brand,
'Come back soon, and carry me away from here.
'I am three months gone, remember, please!

¹ Ping-chou, province and later Imperial capital of Liu Chih-yüan's dynasty was located in present-day Shansi province.
² *Chiu-chou an-fu*, the governor of nine districts of Ping-chou province.

'Li Hung-i and Li Hung-hsin are wolf and tiger.
' "Topsy-turvy" and "Prickle-stick" long since have earned their
evil names!
'I have to stay and face their angry looks and squinted eyes.
'Even the gods here are not at peace,
'And the signs of the Heavens are at sixes and sevens.

'No lie leaves my mouth,
'Whatever I promise, I'll keep my word:
'I am your wife while I live,
'I'll still be your wife when I die.
'No matter what foolishness they may talk
'I'll never heed any one of them.
'I'll never be faithless,
'Meng Chiang-nü will be my model.[1]

7b 'Do not worry! When they tell me to find [another] life,
'I'll shout them away.
'Only when I cannot stand their beating me,
'Only when I no longer can endure it,
'And when it is impossible to escape
'I'll cut my throat or hang myself
'But die I will – somehow.'

She finished her words and her tears dropped like pearls.
Teardrops wet her silken clothes.
She whispered crying, she crying whispered
But dare not loudly cry.
Whoever had blood in him or ate food –
No, even were he carved in stone or iron-cast –
He would be moved.

---

[1] Meng Chiang-nü, the model of Chinese wifely faithfulness. When the Emperor
Ch'in Shih huang-ti (third century B.C.) built the Great Wall against the northern
barbarians, all young and able men were recruited to work on it. Meng Chiang-
nü's husband was among them. When winter came, Meng Chiang-nü wished to
bring warm clothing to him, but she found only his bones at the Wall.

(Coda)[1] She is a pear-blossom drenched in spring rain,
An empress sobbing her grief beneath the moon.
How does she behave?
Like Hsiang Fei, who speckled the bamboo
With tears she shed on Great Shun's grave.[2]

Her eyebrows, even furrowed by grief were so delicate that Hsi-tzu, the Prince of Wu's mistress, had none as lovely. Her face, even drench-ed in tears was yet more beautiful than Ch'i-shih, Han Kao-tsu's love. 'My husband, as long as you are in T'ai-yüan, I'll do nothing but stand by the door and wait for you. Sir, tarry a while, I'll go for money for your trip.' A while passed, but she didn't come back, so Chih-yüan in turn went to look.

(Huang-chung-kung, *k'uai-huo-nien*)

'My wife has not yet come back and she's been gone too long.
'She lets me wait in the deep of night which shows no sign of anyone.'
Stealthily he crept inside and went to his wife's room.
The double doors were locked. He put his head in the window to look.
He saw San-niang.

8a She held a great axe. What did she care for death!
No one lives twice,
So death comes but once.
From ancient times till now
Few had more contempt for death than she.
And even Meng Chiang she surpassed in fidelity.

---

[1] Five reprises of a single melody before the coda are unusual for this *chu-kung-tiao*.
[2] A legend is told that two wives of Shun, the legendary Chinese ruler (2255–2205 B.C.), speckled the bamboo with the tears which they shed over their hus-band's grave.

da) Her tumbled hair lay on the table top
She raised the axe and frightened Liu to death!
Before he could even move – kerchop!

Chiang-nü at the Great Wall was never this faithful, nor was Yü-fei[1] at K'e-hsia as virtuous. But what of San-niang's life?
The blow of the axe had only cut off a lock of her black hair. She wrapped it in a robe of black and violet figured silk, opened the door and handed both to young Liu. 'I pray you'll never forget me.' She saw him to the wall of the compound.

(P'an-she-tiao, *shao-pien*)[2]

When yin and yang first parted to form Heaven and Earth
The separation was very hard,
But do not imagine it was more difficult
Than what this husband and wife did now.
Tonight they cannot bear to leave each other.
Let us exaggerate a little –
They were like Su Hsiao-ch'ing with her student Shuang Chien
    in the post house when she saw him to the River Ch'ien-t'ang[3].
They were as Hsü, the *tu-wei*, surrounded by Sui troops giving

---

[1] Yü-fei, the favourite of Hsiang Yü who struggled with Liu Pang for hegemony in China at the end of the third century B.C. The scene of his parting with Yü-fei at K'e-hsia is one of the most favoured themes of Chinese story-telling and drama. Hsiang Yü perished by his own hand when he saw his battle lost.

[2] *Shao-pien* in its *tz'u* form is known for its great length and prosey rhythms. The singer has doubtless chosen this melody for just that reason 'to exaggerate a little'.

[3] The sing-song girl Su Hsiao-ch'ing and her lover, the student Shuang Chien, enjoyed their deep love until he had to leave and pass examinations in the capital. He did not return for a long time, but Su Hsiao-ch'ing did not want anybody else. The owner of the brothel, however, sold the girl to a rich travelling merchant. Sitting in his boat, Su Hsiao-ch'ing sang sad songs about her fate and one of them she wrote on the wall of the Golden Mountain monastery when they passed it. In the meantime, Shuang Chien became rich and famous in the capital. Once when walking around the monastery, he found the poem and recognized Su Hsiao-ch'ing's handwriting. He found her and happily married her.

his half of the mirror to Princess Yüeh-ch'ang at Huang-p'o.[1]
They were like the Hegemon leaving his mistress Yü at K'e-hsia.
Like the Cowherd and the Spinning Maid parting after the
    seventh evening of the seventh month.[2]
And the rain and clouds parted as they did
When the beloved goddess of Wu-shan left Sung Yü in his grief.[3]

8b 'If sold, my robe of figured silk, can furnish money for your trip',
    said San-niang.
Her generosity is a great as the mountain.
A moment before she had let down her cloud of black hair
And cut off a lock of it with the axe.
She hands it now to young Liu saying:
'Remember often tonight's love.'
Should you recall examples from the past
Of such affectionate partings
I think no grief in all the world
Could be compared with theirs.
Her pain was so great, again and again the tear pearls fell.
The earth was mourning, Heaven was plunged in sorrow,
The sun itself gave no light.
If Buddha of the Eternal Smile were witness, he too would frown.

(Coda) A mandarin duck driven from its mate,
    Lien-li trees cut asunder,
    Uncaring Hung-hsin and Hung-i have made
    The lonely *luan* bird and solitary phoenix separate.

    Hung-hsin was a fence as high as the sky. Hung-i was a wind-screen
reaching the earth. 'Prickle-stick' was the awl to undo their love-knot.

---

[1] See p.48, note 1.
[2] A myth based upon the union of the constellation of the Herdboy and Spinning Damsel, which is supposed to occur in the 7th of the 7th lunar month. The
lovers living in the stars could meet only once a year.
[3] Clouds and rain are symbolic of sexual relationship. Allusion to a famous sensual
poem *Shen-nü fu* (The Goddess) by Sung Yü (third century B.C.)

'Topsy-turvy' was the saw which cut the *lien-li* trees with interlocked branches. The whole day they plan to drive Chih-yüan from their house and cause husband and wife to live apart. Chih-yüan and San-niang had just said good-bye to each other when suddenly they heard a shout.

(Hsieh-chih-tiao, *shua-san-t'ai*)

Li San-niang and Liu Chih-yüan –
A couple who had scarce begun to live together.
Her tears were as many as the raindrops.
'An old grief is seldom dispersed by a new one.'
'When you arrive at Ping-chou
'Send back for me.
'Don't make me wait too long by the door,
'Think often on tonight's parting,
'Sir, recall everything of our past.'

9a

Suddenly there was a loud shout
Which startled husband and wife.
Li Hung-i dressed all differently:
(His face about to burst with rage)
A shiny black turban, his tunic girt by a cord,
Leather boots for which two rabbits had once been brought to grief.
The sash about his middle
Was three feet wide, of ornamented purple silk.
His shirt was woven of coarse hemp.

In his hand he held a club
Which in the past had knocked down five rough fighters.
His ears stood out like dried-out mulberry leaves.
His nose, arrogant, eyes deep set inside his face.

His thighs were big, his buttocks huge,
He had a quick and ox-lipped mouth
Which drank the crudest village wine without a pucker.
He cursed Liu Chih-yüan:
He called his mother a gallows bird
And him a spine-broken pauper
Who had seduced his little sister – just a child.

(Coda) He opened his mulberry-eating, sesame-chewing mouth
With a shout that matched an ox's bellow.
Which not only Chih-yüan trembled to hear
But the unicorn itself would have fled in fear.

Both brothers raised their clubs to harm the future Emperor.
Both their wives hiked up skirts and raced to belabour the Empress.
Alas! The time had not come for phoenix and mate.
How sad! The swallow and sparrow cheat them.

(Nan-lü-kung, *ying-t'ien-ch'ang*)

9b Li Hung-i and his brother fly into a rage,
Their strength was the wolf's, the tiger's strength.
They raise their clubs
And wildly shout:
'You useless pauper! Not content to lose the ox and ass
'You even had the cheek
'To come back to the compound and lead your wife astray!
'Get out this moment and you'll save your life,
'If you wait, both our clubs are raised against you!'

Both brothers were rough enough at all times
And more so now for they could not resist their wives' chatter,
Like a field of magpies all let loose at once.
They insulted their brother-in-law
Until the Hidden Dragon could stay no longer
But had to leave the compound.

Angrily he cried: 'One day I'll come on the wind and thunder
'And carry back my San-niang!

da) 'I go! I go away! I leave at once!'
Chih-yüan watched her and she watched him
As gradually they drew apart.
Both wept:
The one for he was saddened, the other for she was sick at heart.

    Chih-yüan, leaving, cried angrily to the other couples: 'One day
I'll reach my goal and I'll never forgive you!' The brothers laughed:
'When you are famous, we'll snuff up three pecks and three pints of
vinegar.' And their wives added: 'We'll eat three pecks and three pints
of salt.'

            (Huang-chung-kung, *ch'u-tui-tzu*)

10a Chih-yüan shouted: 'Now I am in shadow,
'But as the storm is followed by bright sunbursts
'So I'll return to take my beauty back.
'Then will I show vengeance to my enemies and kindness to my
friends!'

Hung-i and Hung-hsin repeated their oath:
'When you are famous, we'll sniff up three measures of vinegar!'
The brothers' wives added their bit to be unpleasant:
'When you're honoured and make your name
'We'll certainly eat our three measures of salt!'

da) 'Don't hope to raise the parasol of rank
'Nor sit in a saddle and conduct the drill
'If the cold doesn't get you then hunger will!'

    When they had finished, both couples siezed San-niang and dragged
her into the compound. Liu Chih-yüan set out alone on the old path
to T'ai-yüan. Next day, he came to Ping-chou and asked the inhabi-
tants for information. They told him where to find the army camp and
advised him to visit Brigade-general Yüeh Chin. The ranks had not

yet been filled. Following this advice Chih-yüan went to the camp
[. . . .] The ceremonial visit being finished, next came competition in
drawing the bow. Chih-yüan rejected one bow as too soft. The
General, in anger, had the (stiffest) bow of the brigade brought out
from the arsenal to be drawn.

(Chung-lü-tiao, *fu-ni-shang*)

Officers and the commander-in-chief
Watched Chih-yüan and their faces were pleased.
He stood like a pine,
Like a pine he stood,
His body seven feet high, his presence majestic and awesome.
10b All disciplines of military art he had accomplished
And drilled in them for many years.
The time had come [. . .]
To serve his palace and protect his home.

The noble hero drew the bow as though it were but rotten wood,
Displaying well his mighty strength.
His voice rang like a bell,
Like a bell rang his voice
As he thundered his replies
With his back rigidly to the west
And his face squarely to the east.
Whirling the iron mace [?], he makes the North wind blow.
Wrestling, who can match him?
Swinging the mace back and forth
He startles the commander-in-chief.

(Coda) Brigadier Yüeh is nearly startled to death
As he watches Liu Chih-yüan. For it seems as though
An eight-clawed dragon draws that mighty birch bow.

The General saw above Chih-yüan's head a red glow and struggling
dragons twined together. To himself he said with a sigh: 'Someday

this man's wealth and honour will be limitless.' Thereupon he gave him a jar of wine, three strings of cash, and gave him a furlough in the camp. Later he called Li Hsin, his vice-commander, and ordered him secretly to act as go-between. 'I have a daughter of marriageable age not yet betrothed and I seek a husband for her. What I tell you, you must do and I won't admit any excuse.' Li Hsin understood. He privately visited Chih-yüan and told him about the marriage offer from the Brigade-general's [family]. The Hidden Dragon wept and told the vice-commander about his wife San-niang.

(Hsieh-chih-tiao, yung-yü-lo)

11a When Chih-yüan heard Li Hsin's words
He clasped his hands, gave a bow and said:
'My little San-niang in Sha-t'o village is awaiting news of me.
'She cut me off a lock of her hair
'And when I left, she gave me something for the trip.
'Secretly she made me a present of her lock together with her garment of ornamented silk.
'When I'm branded to the army, if I take another wife,
'She surely will hear of it.'

'Today I want to make you a groom', [said Li Hsin],
'This betrothal, our commander is bound he'll have.
'[His daughter's] beauty is the equal of Ch'ang-o,[1]
'Her face surpasses that of Lo-p'u.
'The family would not ask you directly.
' "One remembers present favours and forgets past faithfulness,"
'They said of old and say it now.
'What matter if a principle suffers?
'With a new wife it's easy to forget the old.'

'Already I have a wife, how dare I marry once again?' Li Hsin replied with smile: 'Sir, how simple you are! Sir, don't you know

---

[1] Ch'ang-o, a great beauty, stole the elixir of immortality and fled with it to the moon. Folk legend says she still lives there.

when the camp gate is shut, the General is king? If you don't comply, disaster will be upon you!' Chih-yüan sighed deeply. The only thing left to do was to accept the betrothal gifts.

(P'an-she-tiao, *ch'in-yüan-ch'un*)

Li Hsin delivered his message,
The groom was fearful because a general was his go-between.
Chih-yüan could not escape,
He accepted the betrothal gifts,
With his face contorted in grief and his brows drawn down.
[. . . . .]
11b [. . . . .] who is who.
How can one know [. . . . . .] Ch'in [. . . . . .]
[. . . . .] Ch'i.

His speech now proves deceptive.
Like a needle in cotton,
Like poison in honey.
'No need to mention T'ang Tun-chuan[1] in the past,
'Nor speak of Tsung-tao,[2] who once divorced his wife.
'For now I am more perfidious than Huang Ch'ao,
'I am heartless as P'ang Chüan.
'My heart is a nest of vipers, of scorpions, of snakes,
'I am a Li Mien[3] who joined the rebels,
'I am Wang K'uei[4] who married twice.'

[1] T'ang Tun-chuan and his story are unknown.
[2] Wang Tsung-tao left his first wife because of another woman. The story is told in quite different ways in novels and dramas.
[3] The story of Li Mien is not known.
[4] Wang K'uei, symbol of man's perfidy. He married a sing-song girl who gave him all her money to support him during his studies. When he became an official, he married another. Wang K'uei's first wife committed suicide and her ghost haunted him during the rest of his life.

da) He wrung his hands: 'Far off in your village,
    'Wife, if you can hear my voice,
    'Forgive my ingratitude for your favours
    'But this time I have no choice.'

        The cloudy hair of her head
        He rejects like dust from his feet;
        The tenderness shown on the pillow
        Is no more than an autumn breeze which passed his ear.
        Not only does Chih-yüan break his first vow,
        But will forsake his first wife for the new one.
    As soon as Chih-yüan agreed to the marriage, the vice-commander's
wives, Lady Li and Lady Wang, became speakers for the girl.

End of Chapter the Second

HOW CHIH-YÜAN BADE SAN-NIANG GOOD-BYE
AND JOINED THE ARMY IN T'AI-YÜAN

Chapter the Third

HOW CHIH-YÜAN ENLISTED IN THE ARMY
HOW SAN-NIANG CUT OFF HER HAIR
AND BORE A SON

～～～～～～～～～～～～～～～～～～～

2a (Hsien-lü-tiao, *liu-yao-ling*)

Chih-yüan, the groom, accepted the betrothal gifts,
Throughout the camp the troops laughed and were cheerful.
The couple – predestined lovers five hundred years ago [1]–
Could not avoid their fate.
The man is a P'an Yüeh,[2] the girl is the Paragon of Yüeh,[3]
The mouths of the go-betweens drip honey.

The camp commander's family is delighted.
At their stoves and in the streets they bustle.
Madame Wang and Mrs. Li say, 'Isn't it wonderful!
'Little Miss Yüeh is such a sweet girl
'The flowers themselves blush to look at her!
'The commander was very clever
'To disregard a present lack of fame and fortune
'And make Chih-yüan his "cuckoo in the nest".'

[1] In Chinese folklore, lovers are predestined for one another five hundred years before they meet: a clear influence of Buddhist karma.

[2] P'an Yüeh, a historical personality from the third century B.C. He was famous for his talent and handsomeness and became a model of the successful young man in China.

[3] Paragon of Yüeh, another name for the beauty Hsi-shih (see note for page 45). She was a daughter of humble parents in the ancient state of Yüeh.

da) 'Seeking relatives, choose not persons of high estate
For fear a single generation may overturn their fate.'
This is the way a general chose his daughter's mate.

They selected an auspicious day and hour and Chih-yüan prepared himself again to become a son-in-law. The General gave a banquet and entertained his relatives. The whole army celebrated. When evening came, the Hidden Dragon and the Empress were wed.

2b   (Shang-tiao, *yü-pao-tu*)

All the family rejoiced, husband and wife performed the wedding ceremony.
Red wedding candles slowly burned,
Priceless duck-sensers [breathed] deep, hot fragrance,
Golden lion-perfumers emitted curling smoke.
Upon the mountain of the folding screen were [painted] fish playing in the water,
Painted there too are pairs of love-ducks and *hsi-lai* birds
And trees with twining branches,
And love-knots all done together.
Face to face the couple stood, poured *lü* wine, shared the cup and the wish
For long life and many years together.
This they call 'the phoenix-sipping cup'.

By now the beauty behind the gauze bed curtain
Should be used to blushing.
Her starry eyes reflect her foolish heart.
Taking off her fairy garments
She holds the embroidered coverlet
And conceals her fragrant flesh.
Her bare back delights in the firmness of the ivory bed.
Then her undone hair lies sweetly tumbled on the pillow,
Pulling her coif to one side.

The phoenix presses herself to her mate:
Seductive tones, shivering words and whispers –
From time to time, sighs.
If all the joys in all the world were gathered together
They could not match Chih-yüan's happiness as a groom that
night.

(Coda) 'Who share a happy life are husband and wife.'
One is the Hidden Dragon; Emperor-Founder not yet revealed,
The other, Imperial Second, whose wisdom and virtue still lie
concealed.

    That night seductive tones were heard through the embroidered
screen and sweet sweat dampened gossamer garments. Suddenly the
cock crows on his perch and the bell announces the morn. The door-
keeper reports to Chih-yüan and his wife that once more they will be
congratulated by the General.

3a   (Kao-p'ing-tiao, *ho-hsin-lang*)

The commander, his four subordinates,
And all the officers wished them happiness.
Throughout the camp each man's cup stayed filled.
Chih-yüan cast a glance to the top of the hall
Fearing his father-in-law's questions
For the door-man has come to the side of the dais
Reporting visitors to him. After murmuring quickly polite greet-
ings
He said: 'There are two strapping fellows here, very rough
'And dressed in a village manner.

'Their cotton clothes are sewn with coarse threads
'And dyed a deep yellow colour.
'Their stomachers are dark red, but picked out with crude
embroidery.

'Their leggings are of white cotton, with ox-skin soles,
'Their headbands are glistening black,
'Their speech is very crude, their behaviour coarse.
'They are from Sha-t'o, the Li compound.
'They hold big clubs
'And are looking, sir, for you.
'They call you "Our Mister Liu".'

> So recently married
> Who would expect the villagers to be so importunate?
> Only this day wed
> Who would imagine the compound could know it so soon?

'The divorce document must have been granted,
  'And generous San-niang I'll never meet again.'
Chih-yüan went out of the camp gate to see. But the newcomers
were not San-niang's brothers, they were Li Ssu-shu and Sha-san.

(Shuang-tiao, *ch'iao-p'ai-erh*)

3b Chih-yüan, frightened,
Went forth from the camp to look.
It was neither Hung-hsin nor Hung-i,
Instead he sees Sha-san and Li Ssu-shu.

He bowed and quickly took them into town.
Always he had been fond of these distant relatives
Who were headmen in Sha-t'o village
And had been *san-ta-hu* officers as well!

Li Ssu-shu was Li the Learned's younger brother and when Chih-
yüan settled with his father-in-law, Sha-san was the man engaged to
take charge of their farm. Therefore, young Liu asked what was the
matter. Sha-san said: 'Your wife sent us for news of you and here we
find you are married again!' 'It was a military order, I couldn't help
it', answered Chih-yüan.

(Nan-lü, *i-chih-hua*)

Questioned, Chih-yüan grew all uneasy,
He hung his head and could not speak.
Deep he sighed and long he paused before he told the truth.
'An order given by the commandant –
'I certainly did not want to –
'Ssu-shu, please, hold me blameless!
'Say nothing!
'Don't tell Hung-hsin and Hung-i a thing!

'For those two oafs are so hot-headed
'No matter how much care you use
'They will not heed you.
'Now I'm in trouble don't desert me!
'What they will say is difficult wasn't.
'What they will say is easy was hard.
'When you return to the village
'Give San-niang my greetings whenever you find her!'
 . . .

Chapter the Eleventh

HOW CHIH-YÜAN MET SAN-NIANG AND HOW HE FOUGHT WITH HUNG-I

~~~~~~

4a '. . . I refused to remarry south of the village,
'Because I refused, they cut off my hair.
'My silk gauze clothes they changed for cotton garments.

da) 'Oh faithless, penniless Liu
'[Father and son] because of you
'Day after day I'm plagued and month by month!'

> Tears have dyed her cotton garments red,
> Endlessly lonely, her eyes are weeping blood.
> Her sweet voice cries once and again:
> 'Oh, my son, you have left me, are you alive or dead?
> Answer me husband! Tell me now!'

(Nan-lü-kung, *yao-t'ai-yüeh*)

Joy filling his face
Chih-yüan began to explain, one fact at a time:
'Your son is alive, my San-niang, set your mind at rest.
'That year when snow was falling and frosts set in
'Your precious brother Hung-i, cruel, vindictive,
'Brought to Ping-chou
'The baby's small cocoon of swaddling cloth
'And there he raised a great commotion before both camp and
town.

'Into a deep snow drift he cast the child
'So much did he hate it!
4b 'But in our camp I found the boy a wet-nurse
'And today he is a strapping lad,
'Brows and eyes both gracefully shaped,
'Cheeks ruddy, ear lobes big.
'Yesterday, before the house, in the willow shade,
'He asked you about your life.
'And you thought it strange from one so young
'Who you expected to be unthinking.

(Coda) 'He called you "dear mother"
'Whom he left twelve years ago.
'He said that you knew him but played the fool
'Pretending not to know.'

Chih-yüan finished. San-niang thought a moment and said: 'This is what I saw: Yesterday at the place where one draws water I saw a stripling dressed in a cotton shirt as full of holes as a fish net. That one was certainly he. Oh! Two more months and what will he do for autumn clothing?'

(Huang-chung-kung, *yüan-ch'eng-shuang*)

Li San-niang listened while Chih-yüan spoke.
'Indeed, the child was really there.
'He had a miserable, tattered garment on,
'No doubt his father lacked another to give him.

'Alas, what was laid down in former lives
'Is lived out fully in this one.
5a 'Neither I nor my son could escape it.
'But the two yards of cloth in my skirt are still quite new,
'Let me give it you to patch his sleeves.

(Coda) 'In the camp, you live in poverty, my son,
'At the compound, I am [beaten] and reviled without end.

'Why were we doomed in our last life
'To bow and serve all other men in this one?'

Chih-yüan said with a smile: 'We won't need your strips of cloth,
your son wears garments with threads of gold and many colours. That
youth was not your son. Hear what I will tell you.'

(Hsien-lü-tiao, *hsiu-tai-erh*)

'He came to your compound walking his hounds
'With a falcon on his shoulder
'At the head of his servants and lackeys.
'He had been hunting for sport
'And being thirsty he sent for water.
'Kuo Yen-wei went for it and met you by chance.
'Our son Ch'eng-yu was very startled
'For once he had dreamt of a fiery pit,
'Where he had seen you standing, crying,
' "Take me from here, save me!"
'He thought it was his mother now and called you to him.

5b 'Said he: "Why hempen garments?
'And why your hair cut to your brows?"
'You told your past to him
'And spoke him the truth in all detail.
'He wept two streams of tears
'Then mounted his horse and sped back to town.
'How can you still doubt me
'Asking if your son's alive and well?
'How can you know nothing of him?
'There is no doubt you met him.
'His brows and eyes, his ears, his cheeks,
'His mouth and nose
'Differ from mine only by age,
'For he is just now thirteen years old.

(Coda) 'Mother and child talked the whole day long.
'Your son is the handsome Prince Liu!
'Even your wildest guess was wrong.'

San-niang cried angrily:
'Why do you say my son is a prince!
'Are you, a beggar,
'*An-fu* of nine districts?'
Chih-yüan was afraid that his wife would not believe him
So from his bosom he took an object.

When San-niang saw it, she could not contain her joy. Her husband
truly had become famous and wealthy!
In a trice, his cotton garments turned into brocade.
The straw rope binding up his hair became a golden crown.

6a   What was this object? The *an-fu's* golden official seal. San-niang took
it and caressed it on her bosom.

(Huang-chung-kung, *ch'u-tui-tzu*)

Then Chih-yüan's wits were frightened from him.
He jumped forward and held his lovely wife tightly.
'Give me back the golden seal', he begged,
'Look, the sun is setting red and low in the west!'

San-niang grew flushed and angry,
She chided him for faithlessness and for not explaining all:
'Many times you've spoken less than all the truth
'But now that we're together, I must know each fact.
'You have become a high official – this is not a common thing.

(Coda) 'I'll keep your seal safe enough,
'But why are you surprised I hold it back?
'I want to hear the truth from you – no more lies or bluff.'

Again Chih-yüan held out his hand, but San-niang would not give
it to him. Finally Chih-yüan said: 'You have it, you keep it! Before
three days are out I'll bring to you a golden cap and ceremonial dress.
6b   And you shall come with me as the law requires. But, please remember
what I said about the seal.'

(P'an-she-tiao, *ma-p'o-tzu*)

That day Liu Chih-yüan
Urgently plead with Li San-niang:
'Today, please, trust me, obey me.
'A garrison commander rules all the land.
'I hold the reins of power throughout the state.
'This golden seal of twenty-five ounces
'Must never be used with disesteem!

'As long as I possess the seal, I rule.
'If I had it not, could I accomplish anything?
'Eight characters are let into its face
'Explaining all my trusts and duties.
'Because you spent your life in rustic places
'You know nothing of affairs of state and law –
'Oh, there are so many little by-paths through them
'I've not the patience to explain them all.

4a) 'I pray you, look with care upon this thing.
'Were it not real and lawful
'I could not command the lowest underling.'

   'I'll tell you, husband, why I am holding your seal so anxiously',
replied San-niang quickly.

7a   (Hsien-lü-tiao, *tsui-lo-t'o*)

San-niang then told him frankly:
'Liu Chih-yüan, think clearly on this now;
'Because of you, I suffered both my brothers' clubs.
'But today, we are exalted, raised,
'I feel I must keep and hide this precious sign.

'To sleep alone each night's a dreary thing, you know yourself
'For thirteen years the phoenix was parted from her mate!'

When Chih-yüan heard this, he held her close –
Despite the coarseness of her clothes
Her body still smelled fragrant!

(Coda) Liu Chih-yüan embraced San-niang and they made love.
The earth became their ivory bed, a tree their shade.
The grasses, they pretended, were tapestries of green brocade.

San-niang said: 'We are joined again as husband and wife, so I must
pay you my wifely respects.
'My husband, be kind, show sympathy.
'Rescue me from my hell!'
Again and again she pleaded: 'Please, come soon for me!'

(Kao-p'ing-tiao, *ho-hsin-lang*)

7b Good fortune now makes San-niang ingenious.
Today she commands even commander Liu:
'Tomorrow, take your troops and generals
'And straightway capture our native town.
'But since your words are difficult of belief
'I'll keep this precious seal just to gaze upon.
'No matter what trick you try it will not leave my hands.
'I have thought it all out carefully!

'You are the son of a jailbird, a matchless, lying scamp.
'I won't forgive you for leaving me to keep an empty house.
'If you come late, you need hope for nothing!
'I care not at all that the seal is twenty-five ounces of gold!
'It could be a seal of jade in a golden box!
'When I hear the rum-tum-tum[1] of the pedlar's snake-skin drum
'Going from village to village beating out its sputtering sound
'I swear I'll swap this golden seal for sesame candy sold by the
pound!'

[1] In Chinese the sound is actually indicated by the syllables '*pu-lang-lang*'.

They clasped hands and left one another
Neither could stand the parting.
    Chih-yüan urged her again and again to keep anxious guard over
the seal.

(Hsien-lü-tiao, *lien-hsiang-ch'in*)

He asks his wife to guard the golden seal
And once again he takes his leave of little San-niang.
Off he goes and then back he comes again,
8a Undecided what to do.
'I've had your rainbow gown and golden crown
'Kept with me these twelve years
'And always felt within my heart
'That you must not be made to suffer.
'So please, wait for me!'

Suddenly they heard a great shout echoing like thunder
And then a man rushed up in wildest haste.
His headband was shining black,
His coarse cotton clothes a gosling yellow.
Very tall he was, with a booming voice
And everything about him showed his rude and rustic ways.
In a twinkling he scattered our two love-ducks.

4a) Holding in his hand a club of mulberry wood
(Which could become a 'heaven-defending' staff)
Hung-i strode up and face to face the three of them stood.

      Up leapt his brows
      Like fighting crickets in the autumn
      Out bulged his eyes
      Like ripe mulberries squeezed too hard in early summer.
    When he saw Chih-yüan, how furious he was! 'Once again I meet
the cross-road cut-purse! Once again I find the quack tooth-puller and
seller of fake medicine!' (?)

Alas! Chih-yüan and San-niang can hardly avoid disaster now.

8b   What will be the couple's end?

'You starveling!' cried Hung-i. 'You came to take food from San-niang, but you got none. Now that you are both here, I'll serve you up our left-overs in this broken pot!' Chih-yüan got furious.

(Hsien-lü-tiao, *hsiang-ssu-hui*)

Hung-i served them a meal –
On one thing after another he prodded Liu.
'May I ask you, Master Liu,
'Whether you've enjoyed yourself since you left us?
'I don't hate you, you understand,
'After all, we're relatives!
'Tomorrow is time enough to decide
'If you should stay here with your wife.'

As soon as this reached Chih-yüan's ears
He burst into angry words:
'You swindler, you cheat me again!
'Even a beast would hesitate to act this way –
'An earthen pot of day-old gruel!
'A pig wouldn't eat it, a dog wouldn't look at it!

'What you don't know, Hung-i,
'Is that I'm famous and wealthy now.
'You still think
'I'm no different from the past!'

(P'an-she-tiao, *su-mo-che*)

9a   Li Hung-i was busy insulting Liu Chih-yüan.
Did he know that Chih-yüan now was ruler of nine districts?
He saw him in his ragged cotton dress
And thought of him as usual as Liu the Penniless.

Then, Chih-yüan grew furious,
Anger filled his breast

Could he contain this blind fire?
He gnashed his jade teeth till it seemed they would break,
The circles of his eyes grew big as armlets
And his shout pealed like thunder.

da) He plucked up the pot and roared:
'You chine-broken cur, you family disgrace!'
And from where he stood he dashed the food in Hung-i's face.

Chih-yüan was imposing as the Jade Emperor[1] rising to the Golden
Castle.
He was as terrifying as Rahu attacking the Moon Palace.[2]
Chih-yüan grew furious, San-niang grew frightened – her body
trembled enchantingly.
Shivering so gracefully, what is she like?
Like a priceless flower from the Emperor's garden, swaying in a warm
breeze.
Chih-yüan plucked up the pot with congee, and all of it he flung in
Hung-i's face. Hung-i in rage whistled a signal. Hung-hsin and both
their wives quickly hurried to him. They frightened San-niang to
9b death. She begged her brothers and sisters-in-law to let young Liu go.
Hung-hsin ordered her to return home.

(P'an-she-tiao, *shen-yüan-ch'un*)

Hung-i boiled with wrath,
Hung-hsin burst with fury
And both their wives were soon enraged.
All hemmed Liu Chih-yüan about and scorned him:
'How dare you speak so, brazen beggar?
'That food was too good for your jackass' belly!
'Get this through your head; no one thought to anger you
'Whether you ate or not was all your choice.

'Yet unprovoked you fly into a baseless rage –
'We see your vulgar nature has not changed!'

[1] Jade Emperor, Yü-ti, the Supreme Deity of Taoism.
[2] Rahu, a figure from Chinese Buddhistic mythology. In the shape of a dog, he
devours the sun and moon and is the cause of eclipses.

When all had had their say
They crowded in on Liu Chih-yüan.
But showing no fear,
He stood there brave and awesome.
Off to one side San-niang said a silent prayer
Imploring the gods to help him.
From head to foot she trembled
And grief had spoiled her perfect beauty –
Furrows broke her 'palace brows'.

(Coda) Liu Chih-yüan was courage itself.
And with his quarterstaff defied
Those who threatened from every side.

10a   Have you not heard of Wang Yen-chang of the kingdom Liang?[1]
About his ill fortune being surrounded by five kings? Alas! That brave
soldier with the heart of a ruler was one man alone, of forlorn strength,
so he failed to found his new dynasty.

That time, kings killed their generals. Now, the servants are about
to kill their master. Though Chih-yüan was very brave, his strength
slackened finally and he could not defy them all. This fight-to-death
of five now summons up a mournful wind. So he looks like a cloud-
covered, god-seizing demon. Though surrounded, the battling Chih-
yüan still is not downcast. San-niang standing by, wears a grave but
lovely face, her fear is inexpressible. The four were depending on their
advantage in numbers, they could not know two more men were
about to oppose them!

If you know not when calamity is upon you,
It is hard to avoid an early grave.

(Kao-p'ing-tiao, *ho-hsin-lang*)

Hung-hsin and Hung-i in their fury
Summoned up their wives

[1] Wang Yen-chang, a general during the period of Five Dynasties in the state of
Later Liang (907-21). He was famous for his courage, as a man of honour, and
as an outstanding soldier. He was, however, defeated by intrigues and the superior
forces of five other kingdoms.

Who hurried to them headlong
Oh, such savagery, rudeness, and arrogance!
No painter could depict them!
Each of them shouting loudly
And all surrounding the noble Liu.
Needless to say Chih-yüan was afraid –
Before the likes of these even the *ch'i-lin* of legend
Would be frightened quite to death.[1]

ob They hoped to bludgeon the Hidden Dragon to earth.
What did they know of two heroes standing on the hill
Who saw from afar their *an-fu* in distress?
These heroes took their staves and hurried down.
Nowadays, as in times gone by, men as brave as these are rare!
The bearing of one was terrifying,
The other's face was full of goodness.
One moved like a nobleman
The other displayed an emperor's 'divine spark'.
One of them was Kuo Yen-wei,
The other man was Shih Hung-chao.

> The devilish crowd harried the Emperor
> But they met with the gods who defend the law.
> Just as the monsters who troubled the Buddha
> Were confronted by Prince Ne-cha.[2]

> Chih-yüan is now safe of limb and life
> Though this cannot be said of San-niang, his wife.

But what of the four other lives?

End of Chapter the Eleventh
HOW CHIH-YÜAN MET SAN-NIANG AND HOW HE FOUGHT WITH HUNG-I

---

[1] *Ch'i-lin*, a fabulous, auspicious animal. In the Chinese manner, the male is *ch'i*, the female *lin*. It had the body of a deer, tail of an ox, hooves of a horse, one fleshy horn, and from this reference it appears it was also a very courageous animal.
[2] Sanskrit Naṭa: three-faced warrior prince of Buddhist mythology.

Chapter the Twelfth

HOW EMPERORS AND STATESMEN, YOUNGER AND OLDER BROTHERS, HOW SONS AND MOTHER, HUSBAND AND WIFE ARE FINALLY REUNITED

1a   (Cheng-kung, *ying-t'ien-ch'ang*)

Chih-yüan knitted his eyebrows in worry
But the gods sent two men with Heaven's aid.
As soon as Hung-chao and Kuo Yen-wei saw his plight
They grew furious!
Had they been but a moment late,
Just think, Chih-yüan would have gone to the underworld!

Two quarterstaves storm down –
Hung-hsin and Hung-i, though stronger, cannot cope with them.
The brothers were savage enough, in truth, but
Good anguries for these three men are much too strong.
Among them two were Hidden Dragons,
And one was to be a feudal prince.

(Coda) Hung-hsin and Hung-i could hardly fight longer,
All four were hurt and fearing further attack
They surrounded San-niang and herded her back.

None was more vexed than those four people,
None knew such grief as these two lovers.
1b   The beauty yearns constantly back along the path through the willows,
Time and again the brave youth stares at the smoke of the distant village.

When San-niang returns to the compound, she will surely suffer tortures. When Chih-yüan enters the palace, his wife and son Ch'eng-yu welcome him and ask: 'How goes the day?' And Chih-yüan answers.

(P'an-she-tiao, *shua-hai-erh*)

That evening the *an-fu* returned to his palace
And told Lady Yüeh the whole story through:
'This morning I secretly hastened to Sha-t'o
'And one thing after another became clear to me.
'Her worthless brothers and their wives still live
'And have not stopped their cruel madness.
'The most painful thing to me –
'My wife was always harshly treated there.

'Because of me her body is one open wound,
'Her hair's unkempt, dishevelled; her feet are bare.
'Each day she is forced to draw water, hew wood.
'The livelong time she hulls the rice and turns the mill.
'Who can equal San-niang's faithfulness?
'Years ago they offered her a man from south of the village,
'But her image of a wife
'Was one who would not change her husband.
'She remained faithful still to me.

ᵓda) 'Full of joy at seeing her I mislaid my wits.
'I gave her the golden seal I wear at my waist.
2a 'What hope for me should she barter it away in haste?'

      The whole night long he did not sleep,
      But argued with himself how best to carry off San-niang.
      Next day, near headquarters,
      A sudden clamour arose at his feet.
    The door-guard could not restrain two shouting men. When Chih-yüan looked out he recognized Hung-hsin and Hung-i and asked: 'Whom do you accuse?' Hung-i answered.

(Hsien-lü-tiao, *lien-hsiang-ch'in ch'an-ling*)

Before the dais Hung-i declared himself:
'Have pity on me! Long have I lived in Sha-t'o where
'I seed my fields and raise my silk to get a living.
'Thirteen years past, we took a man
'Into our house to marry our sister.
'His name was Chih-yüan, a penniless beggar,
'A man of great strength and a wicked heart.
'Just because we quarrelled a bit with him,
'He left and joined the army at T'ai-yüan,
'Suddenly deserting our sister, San-niang.
'When she bore his child, we sent it to him.
'Who could be more ungrateful for kindnesses than he?
'In the house of Yüeh Ssu-kung
'He took a second beauty as his wife.

2b   (*Cheng-hua-kuan*)

'Yesterday morning unannounced he came to us;
'We saw the penniless devil and were sore surprised.
'He claimed to be rich and famous, to rule over cities and towns,
'But his clothes were tattered rags –
'Words must fail to tell how forlorn he looked!

'He said he was an officer of the general staff,
'But who could believe a word of that?
'My brother and I would not stand for his trifling
'And soon we exchanged hard words.
'Because of his wild and reckless nature
'He lost his evil temper.

                     (*Hsiu-chün-erh*)

'Out burst shouts like thunder claps
'His wild and ugly face was twisted up in rage.

'The circles of his eyes bulged large as armbands
'And he snatched up his quarterstaff.

'Were we supposed to suffer that?
'Of course we had to fight him back.
'It was hard enough to catch that one alone
'But just outside the village gate we found two more.

'One of them was called Yen-wei, the other, Shih Hung-chao.
'In the fight, they used their clubs too handily –
'Our wives were beaten so about
'That they were laid out chins up.
'And I barely escaped them with my life.'

3a (Hung-i was badly wounded and met calamity,
Li Hung-hsin was scratched and cut both meat and skin.
And both their wives only escaped with their lives,
They almost foundered in the springs of hell.[1])

da) 'Of course, we'll send a deposition for your honour's attention
'And will humbly trust the clarity of your honour's comprehen-
sion.
'We are sure that Liu, the Penniless
'Will be haled before your court.'

   In rage Chih-yüan shouted at Hung-hsin: 'You stupid oaf, open
your eyes and look at me!'

(Cheng-kung, *wen-hsü-tzu*)

But Li Hung-hsin kept babbling, unable to shut his mouth:
'That penniless devil Liu Chih-yüan
'Will be not willing to submit himself, of course,
'I suggest that you, Sir, pursue him and arrest him,

---

[1] Here the story-teller intrudes and breaks up this long deposition.

'Otherwise that beggar's cur very likely will run off!
'Summon the man here!
'And let him take that trip which the law requires!
'Thank you for your attention, sir.'

Liu Chih-yüan gave a scornful laugh.
He quickly called up all his aides,
Ordered them in ranks holding swords
And in one sentence made everything clear:
'Hung-hsin, look at me!' he cried.
Both the brothers gaped, their eyes were frozen open.
And then they knew the ruler
Was Liu, their brother-in-law himself!
Oh, what a cruel blow that was!

3b
(Coda) Hearts shrivelled, brows puckered with fright –
The look of panic on these two men!
Wu Tao-hsüan[1] and Chang Seng-yu[2] could not have painted such
a sight.

> Hung-hsin and Hung-i –
> Little servant imps brought before the king of Heaven.
> Chih-yüan boiling with anger
> Ordered his swordsmen to prepare to strike.
> Fated enemies once met can hardly shake each other.
> When bad fortune strikes who knows when it will end?

Ten hemp-bound swinging swords with ringing rings come down
at once. And what about the lives of these two men? Chih-yüan
shouted; the swords stopped in mid-air. 'Wait until I save San-niang
and seize my sisters-in-law. Then all of them will be given judgment!'

---

[1] Wu Tao-hsüan, a famous painter during the eighth century A.D. He distinguished himself by portraits of Buddhist saints.

[2] Chang Seng-yu, another famous portrait painter of Buddhist saints. He lived
in the sixth century A.D.

(Ta-shih-tiao, *hung-lo-ao*)

Quickly his orders were issued
And in no time at all
Five hundred soldiers threw on their armour.
Ornamented halberds, banners and flags
Were displayed disorderly together.
The Empress' carriage with golden phoenix
4a And several [?] . . . horses with priceless saddles
Prepared for the lady to display her wealth and honour,
To carry the golden head-dress and rainbow gown for her to wear.

While everyone made ready to pass through the gate,
There happened an unexpected thing.
The door-guard hastily reported that
A special runner, fleet of foot,
Had secret intelligence for the ruler.
Now it was time for the *an-fu* to be surprised
And he ordered the messenger to his dais.
The man saluted him at once and said
He must deliver an official dispatch.

oda) The ruler of nine districts stood as though rooted to the ground.
He could not imagine what event had occurred,
But soon cried out as though the sky had fallen down.

Chih-yüan lost his ruddy complexion
And his cheeks grew yellow as old parchment.
Liu Chih-yüan asked the newcomer questions about everything and
the messenger told him all details.

(Hsien-lü-tiao, *hsiu-tai-erh*)

When flags and banners were arranged in lines
And troops stood in their ranks,
When Chih-yüan was off to Sha-t'o

To carry back his wife,
Suddenly the door-guard appeared
4b Who ran up to the dais to report:
'A messenger!' said he breathlessly,
'With a secret official dispatch,
'Brought by special runner to your hand!'
The *an-fu* of nine districts
Called up the messenger, read the dispatch,
And his wits were nearly frightened away.
He drummed upon the table and could not suppress a cry.

Again he questioned and queried the facts
And once more the man told him the tale:
'There are five hundred strong troops,
'Fierce and savage as tigers,
'Who have smeared their faces with ash and mud
'And will not give their names.
'They all surrounded Hsiao-li-ts'un.
'Burning hay-ricks light up earth and sky
'And everywhere are raised great swords.
'A strapping man is at their head.
'Whoever he wishes to seize is seized.
'Every wife and woman in town is crying aloud
'And trying so desparately to escape
'That no one remains to tend the herds.

(Coda) 'Not only silks and brocades have been lost today,
'Every wealth and all treasure were plundered –
'And now San-niang is to be carried away!'

    The good things of this world are frail.
    Rainbow clouds shatter like broken glass.
5a   Who has a great share may become orphaned and poor,
    Who has nothing may yet find honour and wealth.
    Immediately Liu Chih-yüan gave Shih Hung-chao and Kuo Yen-wei orders to challenge two [of the bandit band].

(Ta-shih-tiao, *yü-i-ch'an*)

Liu *an-fu* gave in to rage,
Never before had he been so furious.
His eyes grew huge, his 'Dragon' face changed totally
And his ruddy-jade complexion paled.
He called up Shih Hung-chao and Kuo Yen-wei,
Both came to the dais to salute him.
'You I will trust with the worthiest of tasks
'Which neither one of you can refuse!

'Dress yourselves in helmets and coats of mail,
'I'll give you five hundred crack troops.
'Let the war drums rumble loudly
'Let banners wave and cymbals crash!
'When you meet the bandits, strike them down
'And drive them back into the wilds.
'Use all your lifelong cunning
'And see that your swords take these rebels' heads.
'But by far the most important thing
'Is to liberate my wife
'With every hair on her head unharmed!

da) 'On this my order is very strict so heed me well;
'We all are men of high and chivalrous will,
5b 'You must take the bandits while remaining undefeated still!'

The two warriors acknowledged their orders and dared not delay a moment. To the east, to the west, in every tent soldiers threw on their armour. To the north, to the south, in all the stables war horses were urged into bridles and saddles.
A command was shouted – the army moved off.
Ornamented flags fluttered about,
Men and horses hastened forward when they heard
Three rolls of the war drums sounding out.
Twenty miles from town they joined battle with the bandits.

> Flags and pennons all askew –
> Sun-tzu's military book ignored[1]
> Robes and armour in disarray –
> Jang-chü's military laws forgotten.[2]

Then see the two bandit leaders riding out on their horses like gods descending from the clouds. Their steeds are as ferocious as mountain-leaping, cliff-scaling tigers. When Hung-chao saw them, without calling a challenge he went straight out to take them.

(Hsien-lü-tiao, *i-hu-ch'a*)

6a Hung-chao grew wrathful,
Wheeled his charger, and even with the ground he swung his sword.
From a distance, before his flags, the bandit watched him scornfully.
He seized his *fang-t'ien* halberd, two feet wide,
And flung it as his challenge toward the riders of the other side.
The battle drums rumbled, two armies raised their battle cries,
And the reek of violence touched the skies.

Swords were raised and sparks were struck from them;
Halberds thrust – and in the air pear-blossom-flashes danced.
Back and forth ten times the battle surged;
Then one reckless hero,
Roaring as a tiger roars,
(Even a Naga could not have dodged him)
Stretched forth his ape-like arms
And grasping his rival's girdle of jade
He snatched him from his saddle.

Ten times they met before one of the warriors found an opening. In the midst of combat he dodged his enemy's weapon and grasping the tuft atop the other's helmet he dragged him sideways. Then he clutched

---

[1] *Sun-tzu* (*ping-fa*), title of the most famous book on military art in ancient China. Tradition says it was written by Sun Wu, sixth century B.C.
[2] Better known as Ssu-ma Jang-chü, a famous military strategist and theoritician during the Ch'un-ch'iu period (722–481 B.C.).

the borders of his armoured coat and with his other hand seized him by the jade belt and lifted him clear of his decorated saddle. Both the armies stood and watched astounded.

> The defeated one is like a yellow oriole
> Whose golden wings beat heavy in the drenching rain.
> The victorious one like the white egret
> Whose jade feathers grow lighter in the blowing wind.

6b   Who was the man seized alive?

(Kao-p'ing-tiao, *ho-hsin-lang*)

The bandit was courageous, where would one find his match?
He captured Hung-chao, living, and dragged him back to his ranks.
In his hand he held his icicle – halberd level,
Wheeled his horse about and rode back out.
As imposing and fierce as an enraged Lü Pu[1]
Again, he appeared before the troops and cried:
'You, Yen-wei, hear my words;
'Don't be like this mindless wretch
'Don't wait for me to beat you in a fight!

'The proverb does not lie which says:
' "Who hates must have an object
' "As debt must have its creditor!"
'You must have your strict commands –
'And I don't care if you live or die –
'But in the name of humanity and right I'd send you back
'And trouble you to relay just one speech.
'Tell this to Liu, the *an-fu*, say:
' "Come forth yourself in person and carry back your wife!" '

> When Yen-wei heard it
> His eyes grew wide and flashed.

---

[1] Lü Pu, a historical personality who lived during the Eastern Han period (A.D. 25–220), was Lieutenant and adopted son of Tung Cho, but subsequently became disgusted by the latter's tyranny and helped to kill him.

When he shouted at the bandit.
Anger and hatred dripped like blood from his face and beard.
7a   On his horse he flew to seize his enemy.

(Yüeh-tiao, *t'a-chen-ma*)

Both these angry men feed their madness –
Each struts his bravery, skill, and heroic mien –
They clash in final battle on their mounts.
Alarm sounds of the ornamented trumpets
Trouble the heavens with their din.
The frantic thunders of war drums
Stun the earth with their sound.
The dust is trampled up and dirt rains down from everywhere.
Where arms struck each other, white sparks glanced,

Where divine weapons whirled, cold lightning danced.
Halberd's points struck one another,
For the moment nothing matters but to win or die!
None cares that in a trice he might be covered by the Yellow
Springs.
Long they fought but there was neither victory nor defeat.

(Coda)   You could not tell which was the stronger.
Then for a while they rested before their ranks
And leant on their ornamented saddles atop their horses' heaving
flanks.

In their battle to the finish the military arts of both were equal. Eyes
as sharp as the bandit's are rare on the earth. Deft hands like Yen-wei's
are hard to find anywhere. Fifty times they clashed but there was
7b   neither victor nor victim. Each returned to his side to rest. But alas!
Kuo Yen-wei became too reckless. He deployed his troops before their
banners and tried again to carry off the lady and take her back to
headquarters. The troops once more waved their ornamented flags,
soldiers beat a flourish on the war drums.
    The rest over, strength recovered, the duel began again.
    The hands holding the swords returned to their work.

(P'an-she-tiao, *su-mu-che*)

Both generals rested a while
But then Kuo deployed his troops.
Alas! His heart had grown too hasty!
In furious irritation he dashed for another mount
To measure again his bravery and ardour.

As he hurried to his beast, he saw a messenger;
The man was tottering with fear
And quickly stuttered out his report.
His mouth spoke a terrible disaster!
'Five hundred of our soldiers are on the brink of defeat!'

a) Kuo Yen-wei's courage drained away.
Straight north of them a dust-cloud seemed to boil and sway
And another squad of wild horsemen galloped up.

  Watching from afar they could distinguish nothing
  But guessed that the bandit's reinforcements had arrived.
8a Looking closer
  It proved to be the nine-district-*an-fu*'s cohorts!
In the shade of two hundred ornamented flags – gifts of the Emperor,
in the crowd of three hundred long silver lances issued by the Son of
Heaven, in the glitter of the armour and surrounded by his bodyguards
the Emperor-to-be arrived! The golden baldachin was fluttering in the
wind, but it could not cast a shade upon the Splendid Emperor. Yen-
wei hurriedly jumped from his horse and greeting his sovereign reported Hung-chao's defeat. Chih-yüan was moved and rode his steed
forth in person to call the bandit out.

  As soon as the rebels saw him
  They threw down their arms and dismounted their saddles,
  Lifted their helmets, cast off their armour,
  And hastily knelt before his horse.
When the ruler saw that they had submitted, he asked: 'Who are
you?' And the two men answered: 'We are not the leaders, there is
another who commands our army.' They shouted toward their main
force announcing the ruler's arrival and his desire to be seen. One man
from the bandits' army rode out.

(P'an-she-tiao, *chiang-t'ou-hua*)

8b Thereupon the bandits told their captain all:
'Their commander-in-chief has arrived from Ping-chou,
'He wants to meet his enemy's chief.
'Do not refuse him!'
When they had thus spoken, the flags and pennons parted to make way.
One man rode his charger forth
And all his troops were puzzled.
None said a thing but each was guessing silently –
Their chief held only his silk whip
And shouted his salutations to the ruler:

'Have you been well since we saw each other last?
'When I've come close enough, *an-fu*
'Fix your eyes on me –
'When you recognize my face, you'll be surprised.'
He slid from his priceless saddle,
Threw down his sword,
Dropped bow and arrows
And shed his armoured robe and helmet.

(Coda) Forward came Liu Chih-yüan, his face filled with delight
'Forgive my failure to welcome you first,
'I will now set that right . . .'
And the Emperor-to-be bowed down.
It was a jade column or a golden mountain kneeling before a thief!

The nine districts *an-fu*
Must be the bandits' relative!
If this were not so
Why would he bow?

And how were they related? Those were Liu Chih-yüan's half-brothers, Mu-jung Yen-ch'ao and Mu-jung Yen-chin! They walked
9a forward supporting an old lady: 'This is your mother! Today we discovered that our brother is an honoured official and we came

especially to [congratulate] you. We did not know that we had seized your wife San-niang.' Full of joy, Chih-yüan greeted his brothers and his wife and dispatched a man to the Hsiao-li-ts'un compound to fetch Li San-weng. His sisters-in-law he sent to his headquarters in Ping-chou and then he ordered his officers to arrange a feast. Lady Yüeh herself respectfully offered the golden head-dress and rainbow robe to San-niang. San-niang, however, refused them.

(Nan-lü-kung, *i-chih-hua*)

Then, during the feast
San-niang made clear why she did this:[1]
'Hear me, little sister, I will tell you why.
'I it was who first married our *an-fu*,
'But we have been these thirteen years apart.
'You it was, good, virtuous lady
'Who urged him on to fame and wealth.

'Today I speak my gratitude to you
'My lady, for treating me with such esteem
'That you received and did not reject me.
'Thanks to you my wishes are fulfilled.
'Now I am united with my son,
'I am content to be your servant –
'Even as your slave I could not hope to cancel out my debt –
'Why should I wish to be the leading wife
'And demand the golden head-dress and rainbow robe?

9b
1a) 'I have always led a simple rustic life
'So were I given the phoenix robe
'I'd know not how to wear it nor how to play first wife.'

The ruler's son said to Lady Yüeh: 'Mother, I would value your opinion. Would it not be enough to receive the lady as my nurse?' Lady Yüeh disagreed with him and they politely yielded to one another several times.

[1] Note that material already given in plain speech need not be recapitulated in song but the reverse is seldom true.

(Huang-chung-kung, *k'uai-huo-nien*)

The golden head-dress and rainbow robe
Ten times they handed one another.
Then the son, with folded hands, knelt beside his mother:
'I can never forget, good lady,
'That for almost thirteen years
'You have cared for me so well
'That my own flesh and blood could not have been kinder.
'I thank you for your gentleness and generosity.

'I hardly expected to save my mother from the fiery pit;
'I can scarce imagine her as my father's wife
'Much less imagine you as his second spouse.'
Lady Yüeh asked, smiling:
'How to disperse these doubts and difficulties?
'I admire your mother's faithfulness –
'Of old or today who has seen her equal?

(Coda) 'Why speak of first and second wives?
       'She'll be my older sister. We will share
  10a 'A single mouth to breath the air!'

    When San-niang saw the Lady Yüeh's sincerity, she accepted at last
the golden head-dress and the rainbow robe, but she felt uneasy in her
mind.

(Hsien-lü-tiao, *tsui-lo-t'o*)

Full of joy yet she sighs and groans
Recalling how she suffered in the village.
'Today my husband is highly placed,
'But though he now has fame and fortune
'There lacks one thing which makes all others incomplete.

'Now I hate my brothers and their wives
'With an even greater hate!

'For they cut off all my hair and spoilt it.
'Now, no matter how we may wish it, I've no future.
'He whose lot is grief
'Is destined never to be rich or honoured.'

la) A man of iron would be moved to tears
To see her look at the head-dress on its golden tray.
Only hair too short for the smallest pigtail
Had been left by her sister-in-law's shears.

    She would like to put the golden head-dress on her head, but alas!
her hair had been ruined and reached only to her brow. She could
hardly gather it together, how then could she pin the golden head-
dress on? San-niang turned to her family: 'I have one wish – I would
like Heaven to tell me my fortune.'

(Nan-lü-kung, yao-t'ai-yüeh)

ob With these words San-niang stood up:
'I wish to speak to all my family;
'Please bear with my awkward address
'For I am village born and reared
'And somewhat ill at ease with ceremony.
'To begin with, it was my departed father
'Who asked our ruler to be my spouse.
'Because of an idle quarrel with my brothers
'My husband and I left each other in grief
'And for thirteen years I'd no news of him.

'My life was hard, I was badly used
'Yet I was supposed to be content.
'How could I hope that a day would come
'When young Liu would be mighty and honoured,
'When he would be ruler of nine districts?
'Now I know "when the bitterest dregs have been swallowed
' "Everything else tastes sweet."

'So it was said in olden times and is true still.
'But how *can* I wear this golden head-dress?
'I must ask Heaven to tell me its will –
'If my destiny is to be great,
'When three times I have combed my hair
'Let it be as it was before!'

(Coda) Say not Heaven has no gods!
They showed her she was to be honoured by men –
As the comb touched her hair it grew long again!

Reverently San-niang asked Heaven's portent: 'If it is [my lot] to become the Emperor's first wife, let my hair grow long again as soon as I touch it with the comb. If gods agree I am only to be the Emperor's second wife, let my hair remain as it is now.' Her words finished, three times she combed her hair and in a twinkling it swept the ground. All cried out: 'A miracle!' Li San-niang put on the golden head-dress – Liu Chih-yüan's hopes were fulfilled. Then the Emperor-to-be told Li San-weng [of his wish].

(Hsieh-chih-tiao, *yung-yü-lo*)

All generals and officers, all ministers and men
Cried out around the table
Then ceased their drinking from the golden cups
And whispered quietly.
Each saying to another:
'San-niang is faithfulness itself!'
'She loyally awaited her husband's return!'
'From her, history's faithful wives have much to learn!'

The *an-fu* of nine districts stepped before San-weng
And kneeling, offered him his cup,
Urging him to drink sweet wine.

'In the past, *t'ai-shan*[1], you gave me your protection
'And cherished me as one would a jewel.
'Save your praises and congratulations –
'If you will give up the village, you can enjoy a happy life,
'A life full of pleasure and empty of grief.
'Under my protection your years will last
'As long as heaven and earth.'

San-weng replied: 'Because you and your wife are together again I am happy enough to die this moment.' – Just as they started to drink, they heard a man report that Li San-niang's brothers and their wives were starving. Chih-yüan laughed: 'Well, I had forgotten about them. Bring them here!' The four arrived and spoke.

11b

(P'an-she-tiao, *chiang-t'ou-hua*)

Before the dais Hung-i wept autumn rains
And bitterly, pitifully crying he called the *an-fu*.
A dense and senseless oaf was he
Hoping only the ruler would forgive him his sins.

But San-niang smiled and said:
'My brothers, my sisters-in-law, just think back,
'For thirteen years you acted poisonously,
'And were my husband and I two Buddhas incarnate
'We could hardly forgive your acts.'

But Chih-yüan stopped her:
'My lady please, control your wrath,
'You must admit they are our flesh and blood
'So surely you would not shame them now!
'Brothers- and sisters-in-law, your worries are over,
'Just one thing more you must do for me.

---

[1] Originally the name of the sacred mountain in Shantung province. Because the shape of its peak reminds people of an old man's head, the expression *t'ai-shan* was used for a man's father-in-law. In the text of *chu-ku ng-tiao*, it is used for the father-in-law's brother.

(Coda) 'Eat every speck of salt you promised,
       'Sniff every acid drop
       'If you would avoid a beating, save your skin,
       'Dissolve our life-long grudge and become close kin!'

       'But that was all in jest,' protested Hung-hsin. 'Surely you did not
    take it seriously that day, sir?' The ruler grew angry.
           The ruler's face turned the colour of purple jade.
           The Emperor's eyes shone like glittering stars.
12a . . . and summoned a man to throw them out. Hung-[hsin com-
    plained]: 'Your wife does not treat us in a manner befitting her older
    brothers!' When San-niang heard this she thrust a finger of scorn at
    them:

           (Ta-shih-tiao, *i-chou-ling*)

    When San-niang heard this astounding speech
    Her expression changed in a flash.
    Disregarding the banquet,
    Ignoring the officers
    Heedless of her assembled kin,
    She riveted her eyes on her brother Hung-i, screaming:
    'And who are you to speak of manners,
    'Who treated *me* so foully I shall *never* forget.
    'And you showed nothing but contempt for my mate and me!

    'After young Liu bade me good-bye,
    'I lived in the village for thirteen years.
    '(The most shameful thing you did
    'Was to cut off all my hair).
    'But how many times, summer or winter,
    'Did you feed me enough or clothe me well?
    'I am your sister, born with your blood
    'But you used me as cruelly as you would a slave!
    'Now you're to be beaten the very first time
    'And you quake and sputter in craven fear.

oda) 'Brotherly relations! When last did you care?
'When you flogged me a thousand blows with your stick?
'When you heaped me with curses I could hardly bear?'

12b   When the young prince saw his parents unwilling to forgive, he
knelt and asked: 'Even though my aunts and uncles treated you badly
in the village, you cannot take out your anger on them. Please, forgive
them, father.' San-niang, lady Yüeh and all the officers urged the ruler
as well, until Liu Chih-yüan felt so uneasy about the punishment that
he released them.

(Huang-chung-kung, *ch'u-tuei-tzu*)

Lady Yüeh, San-niang, the officers,
All relatives, the young prince, and everyone feasting
Earnestly and step by step counselled the *an-fu*.
Until at last Chih-yüan softened his angry stare.

The bonds were untied, brothers and sisters were safe.
They all sat down to the feast;
Bad fortune had passed them by.
A moment later Hung-i turned and spoke:
'I am deeply moved that the ruler spared us.
'I regret a thousandfold what I thought of you before.

oda) 'A silly oaf am I and none too bright
'But I know enough to feel a sense of shame.
'So I shall put out my eyes and lose my sight!'

    So saying, he was about to gouge out his eyes when others stopped
13a him and he joined the feast. It was then a servant reported: 'There is
a young man before the gate. He is about seven feet tall and in his
thirties. His brows are thick, his eyes beautiful, and his appearance
handsome. He sent this card with his name on it for your Majesty's
examination.' Chih-yüan took it and looked at it. Then he shared his
joy with his mother.

(P'an-she-tiao, *ch'in-yüan-ch'un*)

When Chih-yüan heard the news
He bowed his thanks but was astonished and startled.
Then he said to his aides; 'Ask him in.'
In a twinkling a young man entered the room
The moment officers and relatives
Saw the newcomer, they knew him to be a noble
But could they know that this man, too, was an Emperor-to-be?

The *an-fu* smoothed his knitted brows,
The greatest joy filled his face,
And tears of happiness rolled down his cheeks.
Yen-chin, Yen-chao, their aged mother,
Questions tumbling from their mouths,
Learned all that had befallen the youth.

For this noble lad was kin to them
And from the same womb as Liu Chih-yüan.
Later, when his hour has come,
He will be Liu Ch'ung, Prince of Hsüeh
And Son of Heaven for Ho-tung.

13b
(Coda) Destinies all have ripened, each moves toward his fate.
Kin and brother here foregather,
Toast their reunion and drink . . . .

Brothers and wives are met again with . . .
the dragon, the Tiger and their ministers now join forces.

(Hsien-lü-tiao, *cheng-ch'ien-k'un*)

Now that the family was reunited
The banqueting began again.
Music sounded all about.
The *an-fu* looked to Heaven with reverence and thought,

(Must not one whose family is united
Thank the gods for his good fortune?)

The nobleman has found his fate: he has won fame and wealth.
He has taken back his wife. They share the joy of their reunion.
He has even joined again his mother and his brothers.
And in a while his fame will grow more splendid still,
For he will use the Emperor's 'We'
And then ascend the golden throne.

(Coda) I was asked to make a new tale from the old.
For this worthy, intelligent assembly
I was happy to unfold
The story of Liu Chih-yüan
From the beginning to the end
And with absolutely nothing left untold.

End of Chapter the Twelfth
HOW EMPERORS AND STATESMEN, YOUNGER
AND OLDER BROTHERS, HOW SONS AND
MOTHER, HUSBAND AND WIFE ARE FINALLY
REUNITED

Survey of *Liu Chih-yüan chu-kung-tiao* editions

1. Cheng Chen-to's edition in 1935. Published in *Shih-chieh wen-k'u*, Vol.2 (Shanghai, 1935), pp.483–508.

   It cannot be considered a critical edition. There are several wrong characters which do not correspond to the original and which alter the meaning of the text.

2. Lai-hsün-ko edition in Peking, 1937.

   Photo-lithographic reproduction after photographs of the original taken by Kano Naoki in 1928 in Leningrad where the book was stored. Contrary to expectation there are rather substantial differences between the photo-lithographic edition and the original, probably due to corrections made in the negatives.

3. Wen-wu ch'u-pan-she edition in Peking, 1958.

   Photo-lithographic reprint made from the original and fully corresponding to it.

4. Michio Uchida's edition in *Tōhoku daigaku bungakubu kenkyū nempō*, 14 (1963), 240–323.

   First critical edition with an extensive and reliable commentary in Japanese.

APPENDIX

The missing sections of *Liu Chih-yüan chu-kung-tiao* can be reconstructed with tolerable certainty by reference to three other pieces of vernacular fiction and drama given below:

Title	Date	Edition
1. *Hsin-pien Wu-tai shih p'ing-hua* 'P'ing-hua on the History of the Five Dynasties – New Edition' anon.	Sung-Yüan	Shanghai, 1954
2. *Pai t'u chi* 'The Story of the White Rabbit', anon.	End of the 14th century (?)	*Liu-shih chung ch'ü* Peking, 1955
3. *Liu Chih-yüan pai t'u chi* 'The Story of Liu Chih-yüan and the White Rabbit' by Hsieh T'ien-yu	ca.1596	*Ku-pen hsi-ch'ü ts'ung-k'an, ti-i-chi* Shanghai, 1954

Chinese scholars have dated the *P'ing-hua* on the *History of the Five Dynasties* as early as mid-eleventh century. If this is so, our *chu-kung-tiao* would form a kind of vector between *p'ing-hua* and drama. Below are tabulated eleven important episodes in the core story of Liu Chih-yüan which are shared in one fashion or another by the four versions we have left to us (Table I). It should be noted that our incomplete *chu-kung-tiao* text is missing from items 4 to 10. By allusion still in the extant *chu-kung-tiao* and by establishing the relationship of the *chu-kung-tiao* story to the others it is possible to reconstruct and verify details of the episodes which constituted the sections of *chu-kung-tiao* text now missing (Table II).

TABLE I

Episode	P'ing-hua	Chu-kung-tiao	Pai t'u chi	Liu Chih-yüan pai t'u chi
1. Li, the elder, marries his daughter Li San-niang to Liu Chih-yüan because he has seen supernatural phenomena over the sleeping hero and knows he will become Emperor.	†¹	†	†	†
2. Li San-niang's brothers chase Liu Chih-yüan away and he joins the army.	†	†	†	†
3. Liu tested in contest of arms. The General sees supernatural phenomena above Liu's head and marries his daughter to him.	—	††	—	††
4. Li San-niang's brothers force their sister to re-marry. She refuses.	—	text missing [††]	††	††
5. Li San-niang is forced by her brothers to do the hardest chores.	—	text missing [††]	††	††
6. Li San-niang bears a son.	—	text missing [††]	††	††
7. San-niang's brothers plan to slay the child.	†	text missing [††]	††	††
8. Child is brought to Liu Chih-yüan in camp.	†	text missing [†]	††	††
9. Liu Chih-yüan's military and civil career after he leaves Li San-niang .	†	text missing [†]	†	†
10. Liu Chin-yüan's son meets his mother by chance.	†	text missing [†]	††	††
11. Liu Chih-yüan is re-united with Li San-niang and his relatives.	†	††	††	††

¹ † episode present
†† episode present in two or more works even in detail
[†] or [††] episode not present in *chu-kung-tiao* because of missing text, but allusions in the present text imply that it duplicates another work in outline [†] or even in detail [††]
— episode not present.

To analyse the degree of similarity between the *chu-kung-tiao* version and the other forms one need only add up the plus and minus marks. It then becomes evident that *chu-kung-tiao* and *p'ing-hua* have seven similar and four dissimilar episodes; *Pai t'u chi*, nine similar and two dissimilar while *Liu Chih-yüan pai-t'u chi* and *chu-kung-tiao* share all eleven episodes.

It is fairly obvious that *chu-kung-tiao* follows the core legend as it appears in the *p'ing-hua* but enriches it with a number of new elements. Logically, one should not use *p'ing-hua* to reconstruct anything but the core of the *chu-kung-tiao*, never the details of any episodes.

Though it appears strange that the sixteenth-century drama *Liu Chih-yüan pai-t'u chi* shares more details with the *chu-kung-tiao* version than does the fourteenth-century drama *Pai-t'u chi*, a careful reading of both reveals that the plots of the two are quite different, that they probably had two different names to begin with and that the later drama did not evolve from its fourteenth-century namesake.[1]

Pai-t'u chi probably drew upon a source other than *chu-kung-tiao*, (possibly on a legend or a literary work no longer extant). *Liu Chih-yüan pai t'u chi*, however, did not elaborate upon the earlier drama but upon the story as found in *Liu Chih-yüan chu-kung-tiao*. It is doubtful that Hsieh T'ien-yu, the author of the later drama, knew the *chu-kung-tiao*, but the tradition of the story as told by *Liu Chih-yüan chu-kung-tiao* could still have been alive in the sixteenth century.

The propensity of the *chu-kung-tiao* narrator to indulge in recapitulations of the plot may often be a source of irritation to the reader but is, of course, the means by which the literary historian can most successfully reconstruct missing parts. Arranging the resources in order of their importance then, we have (a) the *chu-kung-tiao* itself, (b) *Liu Chih-yüan pai-t'u chi*, (c) *Pai-t'u chi*, and (d) *Wu-tai shih p'ing-hua*. Table II, below, is in my view the most probable reconstruction of the lacunae in our contemporary copy of the *Liu Chih-yüan chu-kung-tiao*.

---

[1] In *Liu Chih-yüan pai-t'u chi* the key episode concerns the white rabbit which leads Chih-yüan's son to his mother. The most important episode of *Pai-t'u chi*, however, is the Imperial-red robe with which the General's daughter covers the sleeping Chih-yüan. Since this is the only recension in which such a robe is made part of the plot some Chinese literary historians believe that *Pai-t'u chi* was probably once entitled *Hung-p'ao chi* (The Imperial Robe). No drama by this title exists today but one by that title is alluded to in *Chin p'ing mei tz'u-hua* (ed. of 1933, Ch.66, p.6a).

TABLE II

Reconstruction   Verification

Chapter 1, pp.3–4

Liu Chih-yüan was hungry when he
reached the wineshop, but had no
money to order. Moved by his life
story, the innkeeper was kind enough
to give him a meal. Suddenly a man
burst into the wine-shop. His
appearance was frightful.

Ckt. Liu, Ch.1, 5b, 3: The man who
burst into the wine-shop, was
Li Hung-i, called Living Vampire
by all other villagers. He shouted
and commanded the innkeeper like
a slave. Therefore Liu Chih-yüan
began to fight with him because
*'he still wanted to pay back the old
man's kindness – for he had given him
food to eat.'*

Chapter 3, 2nd half

The headmen of Sha-t'o village
return and tell Li San-niang and her
brothers that Liu Chih-yüan has
married the General's daughter in
T'ai-yüan. The brothers press Li
San-niang to marry a man from
south of the village. She refuses and
to demonstrate her determination to
be faithful to her husband, she cuts
off her beautiful hair.

1. *Ckt. Liu*, Ch.11, 4a, 1: After thirteen
years Li San-niang and Liu Chih-
yüan meet again. She describes her
life to him. *'I refused to remarry
south of village/And because I was
unwilling to re-marry they cut off my
hair.'*

2. *Ckt. Liu*, Ch.12, 10a, 5: Li San-
niang complains during the banquet
about her brothers: *'Now I hate my
brothers and their wives with an even
greater hate,/For they cut off all my
hair and spoilt it.'*

3. *Ckt. Liu*, Ch.12, 1b, 9–10: After he
had returned from Li San-niang to
the palace, Liu Chih-yüan told his
second wife what happened with
Li San-niang: *'Who can be compared
to San-niang in faithfulness? /Long
ago they introduced her to someone
from south of the village/But her image
of a wife/Was one who would not
change her husband/So she remained
faithful still to me.'*

The same episode is elaborated, both
in *Liu Chih-yüan pai t'u chi*, Ch.2,
Act 25, pp.7a–8a, and *Pai t'u-chi*,
Ch.2, Act 24, pp.5a–7a.

Reconstruction   Verification

Angry at Li San-niang's decision, her brothers force her to be a slave in the house. She must do the hardest chores – draw the water and hew wood, hull the rice and turn the mill. She is ill fed, badly used, and reviled.

1. *Ckt. Liu*, Ch.12, 1b, 8–9: After his return from Sha-t'o village, Liu Chih-yüan tells his second wife about Li San-niang: '*My wife had ever been harshly treated there.| Because of me|, her whole body is an open wound.| Her hair is unkempt, dishevelled, her feet are bare.| She is forced each day to draw water and hew wood.| All the day long she hulls the rice and turns the mill.*'|

2. *Ckt. Liu*, Ch.12, 12a, 7n. Li San-niang tells during the banquet how she suffered. She points to her brothers and asks: '*And how many times, summer or winter, did you feed me enough or clothe me well?| I am your sister, born of your parents. But you used me as cruelly as you would a slave| . . . Remember! I got a thousand times a thousand blows from your club.| I was cursed so cruelly I could hardly stand it.*'|

Half a year after Liu Chih-yüan's departure, Li San-niang bears a son (probably at the mill). Her brothers hate the child and wish to get rid of it. They take the baby from San-niang.

1. *Ckt. Liu*, Ch.2, 7a, 8: When Liu Chih-yüan decides to leave his wife and join the army, Li San-niang says, '*I am already three months pregnant, remember this, please!*'

2. In both dramas (*Liu Chih-yüan pai t'u chi*, Ch.2, Act 27, pp.9a–13b and *Pai t'u chi*) the birth of the son takes place in the mill, where Li San-niang works. It is possible therefore, that this specification was already mentioned in *chu-kung-tiao*.

The brothers take the child into camp at T'ai-yüan to compromise Liu Chih-yüan. Li Hung-i heartlessly casts the baby into deep snow. The child is rescued and Liu Chih-yüan finds a wet nurse. Liu Chih-yüan's second wife takes loving care of the child and raises him as her own son.

1. *Ckt. Liu*, Ch.12, 2a, 9–11: Li San-niang's brothers accuse their brother-in-law before Liu Chih-yüan himself: '*He left and joined the army at T'ai-yüan| Suddenly abandoning our younger sister, Li San-niang|. When she bore his child,| we sent it to him.*'|

Reconstruction	Verification

2. *Ckt. Liu*, Ch.11, 4a, 9, 10–4b, 1:
When Liu Chih-yüan meets Li
San-niang again he tells her about
their son's fate: '*That year when
snow was falling and frosts had set in/
Your precious brother Hung-i was
cruel and vindictive./ The baby's little
cocoon of swaddling cloth/ He brought
to Ping-chou/ And there he had to
make a great commotion before the
camp and the whole town./ He cast
the child into the deep snow,/ so much
did he hate it!/ But in our camp I
found a woman to nurse the boy.'/*

3. *Ckt. Liu*, Ch.12, 9b, 7: When Liu
Chih-yüan's relatives are happily
reunited, his son delivers a speech
to thank his stepmother: '*I can never
forget, good lady,/ That for almost
thirteen years/ you have cared for me
so well/ my own mother could not have
been kinder./ I thank you for your
kindness and generosity.'/*

Chapters 4–10

During the succeeding thirteen years
Liu Chih-yüan becomes the Governor
of nine prefectures of Ping-chou province
and Cavalry Commander of the Chin
Army at the northern defences.
Although his province is surrounded
by the Khitans he succeeds against
the enemy and resists the Khitan
Emperor's demand for his personal
attendance at court. He also skilfully
devises intrigues against his own ruler,
Emperor of the Chin dynasty, whom
he dislikes.

In the preserved text of *Liu Chih-
yüan chu-kung-tiao* there is not a
single allusion to Liu Chih-yüan's
military career. Because this motif
is fully developed in all other
literary works about Liu Chih-yüan,
I assume it was elaborated also in
chu-kung-tiao. Moreover, I believe
one or two chapters may have been
entirely devoted to the description
of battles for such contests were very
well liked by story-tellers and occur
even in the romantic *Hsi-hsiang chi
chu-kung-tiao*. As far as Liu Chih-
yüan's civil career is concerned, the
conversation between Liu Chih-
yüan and Li San-niang (Ch.11, 6a,
1n.) makes it clear he achieved the
title of *chiu-chou an-fu-shih*,
'Governor of nine prefectures'.

Reconstruction   Verification

Li San-niang's son Ch'eng-yu grows
into a strapping, handsome youngster,
thirteen years old. His face resembles
his father's. One day walking his dog
with his falcon on his shoulder and
accompanied by his servants and
lackeys he comes to the compound
where Li San-niang lives. Thirsty, he
sends Kuo Yen-wei for water. When
Ch'eng-yu sees Li San-niang by the
well, he recalls a dream in which he
saw his mother asking him for rescue
from a fiery pit. Ch'eng-yu asks Li
San-niang why she wears hempen
garments and why her hair is cut
even with her brows. Li San-niang
tells of her past and he recognizes his
mother. He is deeply moved and
reports every detail to his father.

1. *Ckt. Liu*, Ch.11, 4b, 1n., and Ch.11,
5a, 8–5b, 1–2. After Liu Chih-
yüan met Li San-niang he told her
about their son: . . . *'And today he is
a strapping fellow,/ His brows and
eyes are gracefully shaped./ His
cheeks ruddy, his ear lobes, big./
Yesterday, before the compound, in
the willow shade, he asked you about
your life.'/*
   *'Yesterday, he came into your
compound walking his dog and with
a falcon on his shoulder/ At the head
of his servants and lackeys./ He had
gone hunting for sport./ When he
became thirsty, he sent a man for
water./ Kuo Yen-wei went looking
for it and by chance met you./
Ch'eng-yu was very frightened:/ Once
he had had a dream about a fiery pit,/
Where he saw you standing/ And
crying: "Take me out, save me!" He
thought it strange. He called you to
him./ Said he: "Why do you wear
hempen garments and why is your hair
cut even with your brows?" You made
your past clear to him./ And told him
the truth in detail./ He wept two
streams of tears/ He mounted his horse
and returned to town.'/*

2. Li San-niang's meeting with her son
is elaborated in both dramas used
for the reconstruction. It is enriched,
however, with the motif of a white
rabbit which Ch'eng-yu saw during
his hunt and which leads him to his
mother. I do not believe this was
part of the *chu-kung-tiao*, because
there the meeting is quite naturally
motivated by the boy's thirst.

Reconstruction   Verification

First three pages of the 11th chapter

Liu Chih-yüan next morning sets off for Sha-t'o-ts'un, accompanied by two of his aides, Kuo Yen-wei and Shih Hung-chao. At the compound, they separate. Liu Chih-yüan goes alone to find Li San-niang, his friends watch from a hill. Liu Chih-yüan dressed as a beggar, sees everything and understands that nothing had changed since his departure. His brothers-in-law treat his wife harshly, and she is still faithful to him. Liu Chih-yüan finds Li San-niang, and because of his tattered garments she believes him still to be poor.

1. *Ckt. Liu*, Ch.11, 10b, 1–4: When Li San-niang's brothers discover the 'beggar' and pick a fight with him: '*They hoped to bludgeon the Hidden Dragon to death./ What did they know of two heroes standing on the hill?/ . . . One of them was Kuo Yen-wei/ The other one was Shih Hung-chao.*'

2. *Ckt. Liu*, Ch.12, 1b, 5–10: After his return from San-niang, Liu Chih-yüan tells his second wife what happened to him: '*This morning I secretly hastened to Sha-t'o/ And one thing after another became clear to me./ Her no-good brothers and their wives still live,/ And they have not yet stopped their cruel madness. The most painful thing to me – / My wife has ever been harshly treated there.*'/

3. There is a similar episode in both dramas.

BIBLIOGRAPHY OF *CHU-KUNG-TIAO* STUDIES

CHENG CH'IEN 鄭騫, 'Tung Hsi-hsiang yü tz'u chi nan pei ch'ü ti kuan-hsi' 董西廂與詞及南北曲的關係, *Wen shih cheh süeh pao* 2 (1951), 113–37.

CHIANG LI-HUNG 蔣禮鴻, 'Tu Liu Chih-yüan chu-kung-tiao' 讀劉知遠諸宮調, *Chung-kuo yü-wen* 1965, (6), 480–2.

FANG SHIH-MING 方詩銘, 'Chu-kung-tiao shuo-ch'ang k'ao' 諸宮調說唱考, Literary Supplement *Su wen-hsüeh* No.40 to Shanghai daily *Chung-yang jih-pao* of 12 September, 1947.

FENG YÜAN-CHÜN 馮沅君, 'Chu-kung-tiao ti yin-tz'u yü fen-chang' 諸宮調的引辞與分章, *Wen shih tsa-chih*, 4. 11–12 (1944), 38–54.

——, 'Nuan hung shih pen "Tung Hsi-hsiang" chai wu' 暖紅室本董西廂摘誤, Literary Supplement *Su wen-hsüeh* No.78 to Shanghai daily *Chung-yang jih-pao* of 13 August, 1948.

HATANO TARŌ 波多野太郎, 'Kohon Tō kaigen Seishōki to Chō Shin-itsu sensei no tenkan' 古本董解元西廂記と張心逸先生の点勘, *Daian*, 4. 6 (1958), 1–8.

IIDA YOSHIRŌ 飯田吉郎, *Tō Seishō goi intoku* 董西廂語彙引得, published by author, 1951.

——, *Tō Seishō ibunhyō* 董西廂異文表, Tōkyō Kyōiku daigaku, 1951.

——, 'Tō Seishō no kōsei' 董西廂の構成, *Chūgoku bunka kenkyūkai kaihō*, 2. 4 (1952).

——, 'Kohon Tō kaigen Seishōki ni tsuite' 古本董解元西廂記について *Daian* 4. 8 (1958), 13–17.

LIAO HSÜN-YING 廖珣英, 'Chu-kung-tiao ti yung yün' 諸宮調的用韵, *Chung-kuo yü-wen* 1964, (1), 19–27.

LIU CHIEN 劉堅, 'Kuan-yü Liu Chih-yüan chu-kung-tiao ts'an chüan tz'u-yü ti chiao-shih' 關於劉知遠諸宮調殘卷詞語的校釋, *Chung-kuo yü-wen* 1964, (3), 231–5, 237.

MEN'SHIKOV, L. N., 'O žanre chu-kung-tiao i Liu Chih-yüan chu-kung-tiao' (On the genre chu-kung-tiao and *Liu Chih-yüan chu-kung-tiao* in particular), *Voprosy filologii i istorii stran sovetskogo i zarubežnogo Vostoka*, Moscow 1961, pp.78–82.

OSADA NATSUKI 長田夏樹, 'Tō Seishō bungaku hikki' 董西廂文法筆記, *Kobe gaidai ronsō* 11, 2 (1960), 113–31.

SHEN HSI-YÜAN 沈燮元, 'Liu Chih-yüan ku-shih ti yen-pien' 劉知遠故事的演變, Literary Supplement *Su wen-hsüeh* No.85 to Shanghai daily *Chung-yang jih-pao* of 13 October, 1948.

SUN K'AI-TI 孫楷第, 'Tung chieh-yüan hsien-so Hsi-hsiang chi chung ti liang-ko tien-ku' 董解元弦索西廂記中的兩個典故, *Kuo-li Pei-p'ing t'u-shu-kuan kuan-k'an* 6. 2 (1932), 15–20.

TANAKA KENJI 田中謙二, 'Tō Seishō ni arawaretaru zokugo no yōhō ni tsuite' 董西廂にあらわれたる俗語の用法について, *Tōhō gakuhō* 18 (1950), 55–77.

——, 'Bungaku to shite no Tō Seishō' 文學としての董西廂, *Chūgoku bungakuhō* 1 (1954), 93–112; 2 (1955), 75–100.

UCHIDA MICHIO 內田道夫, 'Kō chū Ryū Chien shokyūchō' 校注劉知遠諸宮調, *Tōhoku daigaku bungakubu kenkyū nempō*, 14 (1963), 240–323.

VELINGEROVÁ, M., ' "Ju-k'ou" ho "kou-ch'uang", Hsi-hsiang chi chu-kung-tiao tz'u-hui yen-chiu chih i' "乳口" 和 "鉤窗" 西廂記諸宮調辭彙研究之一, *Chung-kuo yü-wen*, 1959, (4), 184–5.

——, 'The Editions of the Liu Chih-yüan chu-kung-tiao', *Archiv Orientální*, 28 (1960), 282–9.

WU TSE-YÜ 吳則虞, 'Shih t'an chu-kung-tiao ti chi ko wen-t'i' 試談諸宮調的幾個問題, *Wen-hsüeh i-ch'an tseng-k'an* 文學遺產增刊, 5, Peking 1957, 278–96.

YANG YIN-SHEN 楊蔭深, 'Tung chieh-yüan chi chuan' 董解元輯傳, Literary Supplement *Su wen-hsüeh*, No.36 to Hongkong daily *Hsing-tao jih-pao* of 20 September 1941.

YEH CH'ING-PING 葉慶炳, 'Chu-kung-tiao tsai wen-hsüeh-shih shang ti ti-wei' 諸宮調在文學史上的地位, *Ta-lu tsa-chih*, 10. 7 (1955), 3–5.

——, 'Chu-kung-tiao ti t'i-chih' 諸宮調的體製, *Hsüeh-shu chi k'an*, 5. 3 (1956), 26–45.

YEN WAN-CHANG 閻萬章, 'Chu-kung-tiao ming-mu so-t'an' 諸宮調名目瑣談, Literary Supplement *Tu shu chou-k'an* No.34 to Peking daily *Ching-shih jih-pao* of 9 April 1947.

——, 'Shih "chu-kung-tiao" ' 釋 "諸宮調", *Su wen-hsüeh* No.66 to *Hua-pei jih-pao* of 1 October 1948.

———, 'Shuo "chu-kung-tiao" yü "su-chiang" ti kuan-hsi' 說 諸 宮 調 與 俗 講 的 關 係, *Su wen-hsüeh* No.68 to *Hua-pei jih-pao* of 15 October 1948.

———, 'Chu-kung-tiao ti shuo-ch'ang' 諸 宮 調 的 說 唱, *Su wen-hsüeh* Nos.72 and 73 to *Hua-pei jih-pao* of 12 and 19 November 1948.

YOSHIKAWA KŌJIRŌ 吉 川 幸 次 郎, 'Shokyūchō sadan' 諸 宮 調 瑣 談, *Shinagaku* 11 (1942), 111–32.

GLOSSARY OF CHINESE TERMS

Chang Hsieh chuang-yüan 張恊狀元
Chang Yüan-chang 張元長
Chang Wu-niu 張五牛
Chao Ching-shen 趙景深
Chao Ling-chih 趙令畤
Chao t'ai-tsu ch'ien li sung Ching-niang 趙太祖千里送京娘
Ch'ao yeh hsin sheng t'ai-p'ing yüeh-fu 朝野新聲太平樂府
Che-ku-t'ien 鷓鴣天
ch'en-tzu 襯字
Cheng Chen-to 鄭振鐸
Cheng-tzu yü yao-hu 鄭子遇妖狐
Ch'ien-nü li hun 倩女離魂
Ch'ing-p'ing-shan-t'ang hua-pen 清平山堂話本
Ching-pen t'ung-su hsiao-shuo 京本通俗小說
Ching-shih t'ung-yen 警世通言
Ching-ti yin yin p'ing 井底引銀瓶
Ch'ing-lou chi 青樓集
Chiu-kung ta ch'eng p'u 九宮大成譜
Chiu Wu-tai shih 舊五代史
ch'ou-t'an-tz'u 搊彈詞
chu-kung-tiao 諸宮調
Chu-kung-tiao Feng-yüeh tzu yün t'ing 諸宮調風月紫雲亭
chuan-tz'u 賺詞
Chung-kuo ku-tien hsi-ch'ü lun-chu chi-ch'eng 中國古典戲曲論著
　集成
ch'uan-ch'i 傳奇
Chuang Yin 莊因

Han-shu 漢書
Hsi-hsiang chi chu-kung-tiao 西廂記諸宮調
Hsiang Yü 項羽
Hsiao-pien 哨遍
hsiao-shuo 小說
Hsieh T'ien-yu 謝天祐

hsien-so-tiao 弦索調
Hsin ch'ü yüan 新曲苑
Hsin pien Wu tai shih p'ing-hua 新編五代史平話
Hsing shih heng yen 醒世恒言
Hsüeh-shu 學書
Hua-pen hsieh-tzu hui-shuo 話本楔子彙說
Hui-k'o ch'uan-chü 彙刻傳劇
Hung Mai 洪邁

I chien chih 夷堅志

Jen Erh-pei 任二北

Ku chin hsiao-shuo 古今小說
Kuraishi Takeshirō 倉石武四郎
ku-tzu-tz'u 鼓子詞
Kua ts'e erh 卦冊兒
Kuan Han-ch'ing 關漢卿
kung-an hsiao-shuo 公案小說
K'ung San-chuan 孔三傳
Liu Chih-yüan 劉知遠
Liu Chih-yüan chu-kung-tiao 劉知遠諸宮調
Liu Chih-yüan pai t'u chi 劉知遠白兔記
Liu I ch'uan shu 柳毅傳書
Liu-shih chung ch'ü 六十種曲
Liu Shih-heng 劉世珩
Lo Kuan-chung 羅貫中
Lu kuei pu 錄鬼簿

Mei-hua-ts'ao-t'ang pi-t'an 梅花草堂筆談
Meng-liang lu 夢粱錄

nan-hsi 南戲

Pa-wang 霸王
Pai t'u chi 白兔記
Pei tz'u kuang cheng p'u 北詞廣正譜
Pi chi man chih 碧鷄漫志
p'ing-hua 平話

Shang Tao 商道
Shih Chün-pao 石君寶
Shuang Chien Yü-chang ch'eng 雙漸豫章城
Shuang nü to fu 雙女奪夫
Su Hsiao-ch'ing 蘇小卿
Sung Yüan hsi-ch'ü k'ao 宋元戲曲考

T'ai-ho cheng yin p'u 太和正音譜
T'ai-p'ing kuang chi 太平廣記
T'ao Lo-ch'in 陶樂勤
T'ien-pao i-shih chu-kung-tiao 天寶遺事諸宮調
tsa-chü 雜劇
Tse-chou 澤州
Ts'ui T'ao feng tz'u hu 崔韜逢雌虎
Tung Chieh-yüan 董解元
Tung-ching meng hua lu, wai ssu chung 東京夢華錄 (外四種)

Uchida Michio 內田道夫

Wang Cho 王灼
Wang Kuo-wei 王國維
Wang Kuo-wei hsi-ch'ü lun-wen chi 王國維戲曲論文集
Wang Po-ch'eng 王伯成
Wang Shih-fu 王實甫
Wu Hsiao-ling 吳曉鈴
Wu-lin chiu shih 武林舊事

Yang Li-chai 楊立齋
Yeh-chiang Ts'ui Hu 謁漿崔護
yin-tzu 引子
yin-tz'u 引辭
Ying-ying chuan 鶯鶯傳
Yung-hsi yüeh-fu 雍熙樂府
Yung-lo ta-tien hsi-wen san chung 永樂大典戲文三種
Yüan Chen 元稹